We need to tell what Jesus has done for us…

«Now the man from whom the demons had departed begged Him that he might be with Him. But Jesus sent him away, saying, "Return to your own house, and tell what great things God has done for you."» Luke (8:38-39)

The testimony of how I came out of prison and the Lord saved me from death
«He (Peter) declared to them how the Lord had brought him out of the prison, » Acts (12:17)

«And the Lord said, "Simon, Simon! Indeed, Satan has asked for you, that he may sift you as wheat. But I have prayed for you; that your faith should not fail; <u>and when you have returned to me, strengthen your brethren.</u>"» Luke (22:31-32)

«Many, O Lord my God, are Your wonderful works which You have done; and Your thoughts toward us cannot be recounted to You in order; <u>if I would declare and speak of them, they are more than can be numbered.</u> » Psalms (40:5)

My experience and testimony during the month of February in the year 2003 in the Hakimieh Iraqi intelligence prison during the reign of President Saddam Hussein and how the Lord brought me out of prison by Christ appearing in a vision to a Muslim friend (Sheikh) imprisoned with me, declaring that He will get me out of prison and the full realization of the vision.

Some of the Bible verses used are from the New King James Version of the Bible in addition to the use of the Amplified Bible translation for further clarification.

All verses quoted from God's word – The Holy Bible are typed in a ***bold italic*** font

Forgetfulness is the number one enemy of believers in Christ, therefore, *«"My mouth shall <u>tell</u> of Your righteousness and Your salvation all the day, for I do not know their limits. I will go in the strength of the Lord God; I will make <u>mention</u> of Your righteousness, of Yours only. O God, You have taught me from my youth; and to this day I <u>declare</u> Your wondrous works. Now also when I am old and gray headed, O God, do not forsake me, until <u>I declare Your strength to this generation, Your power to everyone who is to come."» Psalms (71: 15-18)*

"I will mention the loving kindnesses of the Lord and the praises of the Lord, according to all that the Lord has bestowed on us ..." Isaiah 63: 7

Dear reader, I am sure that you also have many testimonies that the Lord has already done in your life personally and where you have seen the hand of the Lord working hard, and perhaps you did not pay attention to it properly or did not pay enough attention to write it down to be as a documented history of God's hands in your personal life.

I encourage you to do this to encourage yourself and others around you and to testify through these testimonies the power of the active and living Word of God that has been working in the past and is working today in our present generation and will also work in the future in the lives of everyone who believes in it.

"... that I may be encouraged together with you by Titus 1:4the mutual faith both of you and me", Romans 1: 12

Acknowledgments

I extend my sincere thanks and appreciation to my Lord, my God and my Savior Jesus Christ, who has never abandoned me despite all my weaknesses, failures, doubts and sins. To me, He is truly my God, friend, brother and everything in life, while I am only a body. He will remain faithful to me even after I leave this temporary body when I am given a heavenly body to be with Him, as He promised me and all who believe in Him in the ***Epistle to the Philippians (3: 20-21) «"For our citizenship is in heaven, from which we also eagerly wait for the Savior, the Lord Jesus Christ, who will transform our lowly body that it may be conformed to His glorious body, according to the working by which He is able even to subdue all things to Himself."»*** Yes, that is also His promise to everyone who believes in Him.

Here also, I would like to thank my precious dear wife, who has labored with me greatly, for her patience and bearing, and who has truly been a helper despite all the tribulations, troubles, storms and endless evils our marriage has encountered. The Lord has helped us until now and has given us grace to stand firm and declare what He has done in our lives. May all glory be given to Him forever, Amen.

In addition, I would like to thank my honorable and beloved local church pastor **Rev. Gregory Dickow**, church pastor of **Life Changers International Church** in Illinois in the United States of America. The Lord has used him forcefully in my life in the reconciliation of my relationship with Lord Jesus again after a long journey of pain, conflict and lack of clear understanding of the word of God from God's point of view, and which in turn, led to a stumbling relationship with the Lord and behaving in a manner that is not according to God's will for my life. By that, I mean behaving as person trying to uselessly please God religiously, all the while forgetting that God does not want or expect me to do any works for Him except have faith and persevering in grace and faith in the One who fully did the will of God and complete work on the cross, namely Jesus Christ, His son.

However, the Lord's faithfulness did not forsake me or abandon me even when I had wandered away from Him; rather He searched for me and found me because He is faithful and cannot deny Himself as He promised in His word, the Bible, and as He promised me as well; that He shall search for me by appointing a pastor according to His heart to look after me regarding knowledge and understanding. He also promised in the ***Book of Jeremiah (3: 15) «"And I will give you shepherds according to my heart, who will feed you with knowledge and understanding."»***

Special thanks and appreciation also to the humble and faithful servant of the Lord brother Larry Chkoreff, who has been my friend for many years without seeing him face to face, but I saw his heart and knew his character through my communication with him through various means of communication and the leadership of the Holy Spirit. Special thanks and appreciation to him for his continuous encouragement to me and his continued willingness to provide the help and advice that emanates from his heart towards me to publish this book.

Special thanks and heartfelt appreciation to all members of my family, my mother and my brothers, and to all the brothers and sisters in Iraq and around the world who prayed for us in our distress for the liberation of the Lord and declared and proved practically that we are all members of one body through their love and prayers for us.

"For just as we have many parts in one body—and all the parts do not have the same function — so we, who are many, are one body in Messiah and everyone parts of one another.", Romans 12: 4-5 TLV

"And if one member suffers, all the members suffer with it; or if one member is honored, all the members rejoice with it. Now you are the body of Christ, and members individually." 1ˢᵗ Corinthians 12: 26-27

Thanks to all of you

Why did I write this book?

I never thought of writing this book or publishing any of this before. The idea at first was just to remember the merciful and miraculous work God had done in my life as I seem to forget quickly as soon as adversity hits and new trials that I haven't faced before come up. So, I decided to put everything God has done for me on paper, so I would remind myself and never forget Who (God) is with me and think only of who is against me (Satan, the world, sin, the flesh, problems, adversity, trials people around me and even myself and my past). For, *«"What then shall we say to these things? If God is for us, who can be against us?"» Romans (8:31)* The idea then grew and I decided to write for my children as well, so they may know what God has done in my life as their father even after I am gone to be with whom my heart loves forever (Lord Jesus Christ who loved to death). Later, it evolved into composing these testimonials into a documented book and then publishing it in two or more languages. That is how the idea of writing a book, which never occurred to me before, came together.

1. To give glory to the Lord Jesus Christ as well as His faithfulness and the power of His word

The purpose of this testimony is to give all glory to the Lord Jesus Christ and to testify and declare that He was, is and always will be alive, faithful as well as protector, defender, mediator and helper to all of us believers here on Earth and in eternal life as well, as the bible declares *«"Our soul waits for the Lord; He is our help and our shield."» Psalms (33:20)* , and that His word is alive, active and remains forever, and that He is faithful to us regardless of our lack of faithfulness to Him *«" If we are faithless, He remains faithful; He cannot deny Himself."» 2 Timothy (2:13)*, and that He shall keep us and our faith in Him until the end because of His love and faithfulness towards us *«"But I have prayed for you, that your faith should not fail"» Luke (22:32)*

2. To document what the Lord has done in my life

Also, to document what the Lord has done in my life in a few pages available for everyone to read, so that this testimony is not exclusive to some relatives or certain group of people, *«"I have proclaimed the good news of righteousness in the great assembly; indeed, I do not* *restrain my lips, O Lord, You Yourself know. I have not hidden Your righteousness within my heart; I have declared Your faithfulness and Your salvation; I have not concealed Your loving-kindness and Your truth from the <u>great assembly.</u>"» Psalms (40: 9-10)*

3. <u>**To learn some basic principles in trials and to stand firm in God's living and active word**</u>

   In addition to learning some basic principles about the trials we currently face and will face in the future, and to hold on to the God's promises that He has declared in His word (the Holy Bible), which will timely turn into living words and experiences in our lives.

4. <u>**A message of comfort, encouragement and readiness for believers in Jesus Christ**</u>

   This is also a message of comfort and encouragement for every persecuted, maltreated or imprisoned believer for his faith in Christ at current times or in the future, as well as the readiness of the church for the coming of Christ and the oppression that will precede His coming that is practically at the door and very near. Every believer must realize that he is not a victim on Earth for whomever so wishes him to be; rather to know that he is carefully protected by God the Father Himself, and that a hair shall not fall from his head except by His permission, as the Bible declares *«"And do not fear those who kill the body but cannot kill the soul. But rather fear Him who is able to destroy both soul and body in hell. Are not two sparrows sold for a copper coin? And not one of them falls to the ground apart from your Father's will. <u>But the very hairs of your head are all numbered.</u> Do not fear therefore; you are of more value than many sparrows."» Matthew (10: 28-31)*. If it happens that a believer in Christ is killed, (although not all believers are called to achieve this great honor since not one of us deserves) it is not the end of him, rather a transition phase from the state of flesh to the state of spirit, the beginning of the most wonderful face to face relationship with our Lord *«"…, but we know that when He is revealed, we shall be like Him, for we shall see Him as He is."» 1 John (3:2)*. Even more, believers should pray even for those who want to kill us, because physical death is not the end for a believer, but the body we live in now represents a barrier making us absent from God, as the Bible states *«"So we are always confident, knowing that while we are at home in the body we are absent from the Lord."» 2 Corinthians (5:6)*. And *«"For to me, to live is Christ, and to die is gain."» Philippians (1:21)* Therefore, do not worry my dear believer, for you believe in the One who said He is the resurrection and life, and whoever so believes in Him shall live even after death *«"Jesus said to her, "I am the resurrection and the life. He who believes in Me, though he may die, he shall live"."» John (11:25)*, you believe in the One who has the keys to the pit and death *«"... saying to me "Do not be afraid; I am the First and the Last. I am He who lives, and was dead, and behold, I am alive forevermore. Amen. And I have the keys of Hades and of Death."» Revelation (1: 17-18)*. So, be calm and enjoy God's peace which surpasses any other *«"and the peace of God, which surpasses all understanding, will guard your hearts and minds through Christ Jesus."» Philippians (4:7)*

5. A message for anyone who wants to know Christ personally

This is also a message for anyone who wants to know Christ personally and to realize that Christ is not a new religion to join or a ritual to practice to be a Christian or even a meeting at church on Sunday to go to; rather He is a person and a real living God that loved you and gave up His life for you, and that He will come again soon to rapture believers to be with Him as He promised in His word *«" I go to prepare a place for you. And if I go and prepare a place for you, I will come again and receive you to myself; that where I am, there you may be also."» John (14:2-3)*

Dear reader, it is your chance now to obtain and experience this promise, to be with Christ forever when He very shortly comes again to Earth as promised *«"He who testifies to these things says, "Surely I am coming quickly"."» Revelation (22:20)* I pray for you to open the doors of your heart to Him and His word today *«"Today, if you will hear His voice, do not harden your hearts."» Hebrews (4:7)*

6. <u>This experience has not happened coincidentally</u>

Another reason for writing and documenting this experience is that this testimony has not happened by chance, but for a specific purpose and a specific day as this; to glorify Lord Jesus Christ and so that the reader may know who the real living Jesus is in the midst of persecution and the fire of trials today. Additionally, the reader may come to know the power of His authority in present time and that He has shared it with us who believe in Him. Jesus Christ is not exclusive to Jonah in the whale's belly, or Daniel in the lion's den, or the three young men in the furnace of fire, rather He is ours, believers in Him, today also in the midst of the fires of life.

The Lord has permitted such a testimony to declare Himself more clearly in order to console and encourage believers in His name as well as those who shall believe because of this message.

Dearest believer in Jesus Christ: You do not believe in a well-known or good-works religion, rather you believe in a fixed rock which will not be shaken forever even if you happen to stagger. So, do not worry, for you are not the axis of this universe. Do not rely on yourself or your weaknesses or sins or fears or abilities or various personal relationships, not even on your past, for your lack of consistency does not change His persistence towards you, as He was with me, and still is even now, and will be forever as the Bible declares *«"He also brought me up out of a horrible pit, out of the miry clay, and set my feet upon a rock, and established my steps."» Psalm (40:2)*

7. **The complaint of the enemy, Satan, on my conscience and his attempts to destroy me in every way**

   I would like to add that the devil has tried all his power to kill me and destroy my life in every way he could, just as the bible says *«"For innumerable evils have surrounded me; my iniquities have overtaken me, so that I am not able to look up; they are more than the hairs of my head;*

therefore my heart fails me."» Psalm (40:12). My lack of clear knowledge of the word of God, and my weaknesses, failures, past, fears, and personal sins were used by Satan to constantly accuse me, whether day or night, through guilt and condemnation, which is what he also does with you, O believer in Christ as the Bible declares «*" Then I heard a loud voice saying in heaven, "Now salvation, and strength, and the kingdom of our God, and the power of His Christ have come, <u>for the accuser of our brethren, who accused them before our God day and night, has been cast down."</u>» Revelation (12:10)* He also constantly planted seeds of doubt in my life, until finally, I even doubted my faith in the Lord Jesus which the Bible mentions «*"And the Lord said, "Simon, Simon! Indeed, Satan has asked for you, that he may sift you as wheat. <u>But I have prayed for you; that your faith should not fail; and when you have returned to Me, strengthen your brethren".</u>» Luke (22: 31-32)* In addition to the many life threatening risks that I faced before and during the war on Iraq, from explosions to street fighting with live heavy artillery to drowning and even exposure to deadly electrical shocks, not to mention his repeated attacks on my home and family to try to destroy my life and my family's life as well. In addition to the many hardships I endured at the hands of so-called "brethren" (false brethren) and the frequent threats of death I previously got. This enemy, Satan, has done all he could do so that I may not speak of what the Lord has done in my life, just as it is written *«"You pushed me violently, that I might fall, but the Lord helped me. The Lord is my strength and song, and He has become my salvation."» Psalm (118: 13-14) «"For this is God, our God forever and ever; He will be our guide even to death."» Psalm (48:14)* However, I am here today, to tell you what the Lord has done for me and what He has planned to also do for you if you believe in Him, *«"Jesus said to him, "If you can believe, all things are possible to him who believes"."» Mark (9:23)*

I do not claim that I am perfect or pure or that I do not sin, not at all "", but I am human, with weaknesses, failures and personal sins that I still suffer from because *«"For the flesh lusts against the Spirit, and the Spirit against the flesh; and these are contrary to one another, so that you do not do the things that you wish."» Galatians (5:17)* I do, however, believe in the One who is whole i.e. Jesus, and His complete work for me on the cross, while at the same time I am captivated in pursuing perfection as the Apostle Paul said in his epistle to the Philippians *«"Not that I have already attained, or am already perfected; but I press on, that I may lay hold of that for which Christ*

Jesus has also laid hold of me. Brethren, I do not count myself to have apprehended; but one thing I do, <u>forgetting those things which are behind and reaching forward to those things which are ahead, I press toward the goal for the prize of the upward call of God in Christ Jesus"»</u> Philippians (3: 12-14) God is still continuously working inside me and on my character in temporary stages in my life and the lives of every believer in Christ simply for the fact that what we cannot get rid of today, we will be able to let go tomorrow and so on. Therefore, His ultimate goal, for me and all believers on Earth, is to resemble His son Jesus. A calling for any believer who has been chosen in Christ; to resemble His son Jesus, as the Apostle Paul declares in his epistle to Romans *«"For whom He foreknew, He also predestined to be conformed to the image of His Son, that He might be the firstborn among many brethren"»* Romans (8:29)

What has kept me steadfast to this day despite everything?

The only thing that has kept me steadfast to this day despite all the hardships in my life is not my personal strength or anything else but **The Rock**. **Jesus** is the rock that I believe in from the beginning, as the bible states *«"Jesus said to her, "I am the resurrection and the life. He who believes*

in Me, __though he may die, he shall live__". "» John (11:25)
Alike, whoever builds his life on Jesus, will be fixed in
Him because he has constructed his life on the rock that
will never shake as the Bible declares *«"The Lord is __my__*
__rock__ and my fortress and my deliverer; my God, my
strength, in whom I will trust; my shield and the horn of
my salvation, my __stronghold.__"» Psalm (18:2)

«"Therefore whoever hears these sayings of Mine, and
does them, I will liken him to a wise man who built his
house on the rock: and the rain descended, the floods
came, and the winds blew and beat on that house; and it
did not fall, for it was founded on the rock."» Matthew (7:
24-25)

«*"I SHALL NOT DIE, BUT LIVE, AND DECLARE THE WORKS OF THE LORD. THE LORD HAS CHASTENED ME SEVERELY, BUT HE HAS NOT GIVEN ME OVER TO DEATH."*»
PSALM (118: 17-18)

The moment I got arrested

On February 1, 2003 the Iraqi intelligence agency arrested me along with a group of Christian believers –around 12 people – for reasons that were unclear, but later turned out to be our faith and sharing it with others and was for our good and for the glory of Lord Jesus, and at that time I was 24 years old and about 3 years in faith since I was saved through the blood of the Lord Jesus Christ in December 1999.

How did the arrest take place?

We were preparing for a worship service in a hall for events in Baghdad, and the number of those present was around 100 people. When we began worship and singing, a group of people, wearing civilian clothes and carrying weapons, came in and assumed to surround the building and everyone in the hall. Then, they began to call out specific names – 12 names – to arrest them one after the other. I was one of them.

We were led into a medium-sized van surrounded by armored cars, and the doors were closed making the inside extremely dark. The driver was driving insanely fast, as if he had found a prey and was exhilarated by it.

Our arrival to the Hakimieh General Iraqi Intelligence headquarters in Baghdad

After our arrival at the headquarters, I quickly realized that we were at the Hakimieh Iraqi intelligence building in Baghdad because a few years earlier I had been a student at a middle-school adjacent to that building but I knew nothing of its importance. I had watched it being bombed by US forces in 1991 when they first launched their offensive on Baghdad and destroyed it by military airplanes at the time.

After letting us out of the car, we were led to the lower part of the building and were not allowed to lift our heads to see our surroundings. We were placed in solitary rooms and kept apart. Two intelligence officers came and said to me, "If you do not confess everything today, we will put you in a casket and send you to your family dead". I asked, "What am I supposed to confess?" They attacked me and tried to hurt me with all their strength, but praise God who gave me grace at the time and saved me from their hands.

Before entering the cell, sitting on the floor hand coughed, facing the wall, waiting what will become of me, I felt like God wasn't with me at all and that He had disappeared. He left me to go through this rough and bitter trial alone. I was completely wrong back then because I was feeling exactly how the bible describes it, *«"Why do You stand afar off, O Lord?*

Why do You hide in times of trouble?"» Psalm (10: 1)

Entering the cell

The moment I entered into that dim-lighted cell, I profoundly realized something in my heart; <u>"I will come out of prison and these people are in deep trouble for arresting us"</u> because we were innocent and hadn't done anything that deserves death or even imprisonment. Personally, I didn't understand why I had such a strong feeling, when a prisoner asked me "What is your charge, and why are you here?" I replied, "I don't know why I am here, but they will be in trouble for arresting us" And they gave me a strange look.

I was in small cell that was hardly enough for all six of us. We slept on the floor and each of us had two blankets, one to sleep on, and the other to cover himself at night. We couldn't tell day from night, but we knew the time by the meals that they gave us and the Muslim prayers. We all used our hands to eat from one plastic plate since metal objects were not allowed inside this particular prison to avoid suicides which prisoners would wish for under torture, beating, and killings they had to face every day.

The false accusations against me and the brethren

My relationship with the men in my cell was good. None of them were Christians but I liked them because even now, I am not bias against the religious belief of anyone. I will not fight someone even if I disagree with them in ideology and belief; rather I still fight my personal thoughts that are not according to God's word – the Holy Bible, by renewing my mind to fit God's word. I was their friend. One day an intelligence officer summoned me for questioning and said that he will kill all of us, Christians, that is, if we didn't confess everything. They accused us of many false accusations without any evidence whatsoever, ***"When he had come, the Jews who had come down from Jerusalem stood about and laid many serious complaints against Paul, <u>which they could not prove</u>, while he answered for himself, "Neither against the law of the Jews, nor against the temple, nor against Caesar have I offended in anything at all", the book of Acts 25: 7-8.*** Later, I realized that they had arrested us because of our faith in Christ and share it with others. All I can say to that is what Jesus said while He was here on Earth, ***«"<u>Blessed are you when they revile and persecute you, and say all kinds of evil against you falsely</u> for My sake. Rejoice and be exceedingly glad, for great is your reward in heaven, for so they persecuted the prophets who were before you."» Matthew (5: 11-12)*** and as the Bible also states *«"All my bones shall say, "Lord, who is like You, delivering the poor from him who is too strong for him, Yes, the poor and the needy from him who plunders him?" Fierce witnesses rise up; they ask me things that I do not know."» Psalm (35:10-11)* When they claimed that they had evidence against me - *«"Fierce witnesses rise up; They ask me things that I do not know."» Psalm (35: 11)* - I replied, "If you can show me one proof of anything you accuse me of, I will sign my execution certificate myself." The bible says, *«"They also opened their mouth wide against me, and said, "Aha, aha! Our eyes have seen it." This You have seen, O Lord; do not keep silence. O Lord, do not be far from me. Stir up Yourself, and awake to my vindication, to my cause, my God and my Lord. Vindicate me, O Lord my God, according to Your righteousness; and let them not rejoice over me. Let them not say in their hearts, "Ah, so we would have it!" Let them not say, "We have swallowed him up." Let them be ashamed and brought to mutual confusion who rejoice at my hurt; let them be clothed with shame and dishonor who exalt themselves against me. Let them shout for joy and be glad, who favor my righteous cause; and let them say continually, "Let the Lord be magnified, who has pleasure in the prosperity of His servant".”» Psalm (35: 21-27)*

An important notice: I admit that I do not hold a grudge against any of them, and that I have forgiven them every injustice and mistreatment they have done to me completely. Moreover, I am grateful for them and thanking of them from the bottom of my heart, because this experience has helped build my life for the better through wonderful lessons. I would like to thank all of them if they are still alive (or at least a few of them that quickly fled to other countries) for the chance they gave me to see God's glory revealed powerfully. That is not just for myself, it is also for many around me, as the Bible says, *«"And we know that all things work together for good to those who love God, to those who are the called according to His purpose."» Romans (8:28)* unfortunately, (like any other anti-Christ state which He loved and died for) they had sewed a few spies, like Judah, in every evangelical church that preaches the truth in Jesus' name. *«"So they watched Him, and sent spies who pretended to be righteous, that they might seize on His words, in order to deliver Him to the power and the authority of the governor."» Luke (20: 20)* A fact that is not entirely new, because if Judah deceived his master, then we aren't better than He is as the Bible declares *«"A disciple is not* *above his teacher, nor a servant above his master. It is enough for a disciple that he be like his teacher, and a servant like his master. If they have called the master of the house Beelzebub, how much more will they call those of his household!"» Matthew (10:24-25)*

They felt that our faith as well as sharing it with others was threatening to them and the security of the country. I explained to the intelligence officers once the fact that Christians respect the state and laws simply because the Bible teaches so, and that there isn't any other book on Earth that teaches such things except for the Bible, explaining to them as follows *«"Let every soul be subject to the governing authorities. For there is no authority except from God, and the authorities that exist are appointed by God. Therefore whoever resists the authority resists the ordinance of God, and those who resist will bring judgment on themselves. For rulers are not a terror to good works, but to evil. Do you want to be unafraid of the authority? Do what is good, and you will have praise from the same. For he is God's minister to you for good. But if you do evil, be afraid; for he does not bear the sword in vain; for he is God's minister, an avenger to execute wrath on him who practices evil. Therefore you must be subject, not only because of wrath but also for conscience' sake. For because of this you also pay taxes, for they are God's ministers attending continually to this very thing. Render therefore to all their due: taxes to whom taxes are due, customs to whom customs, fear to whom fear, honor to whom honor."»* **Romans (13: 1-7)** only then, did they seem at ease.

The Word of God teaches us in **Titus 3: 1 to "Remind them (All people) to be subject to rulers and authorities, to obey, to be ready for every good work"**, Also, not to rebel against the governments *"My son, [reverently] fear the Lord and the king, and do not associate with those who are given to change [of allegiance, and are revolutionary]", Proverbs 24: 21.*

«"For there is no faithfulness in their mouth; their inward part is destruction; their throat is an open tomb; they flatter with their tongue. Pronounce them guilty, O God! Let them fall by their own counsels; Cast them out in the multitude of their transgressions, For they have rebelled against You."» Psalm (5: 9-10)

Testifying my personal experience with Christ

One day, they summoned me for investigation and one of the officers threatened me, "If you do not confess everything today we will skin you." I replied, "I will honestly tell you what I know and nothing more. I am willing to sign and testify to my statement." They said, "You must take an oath that you will tell the truth." I told them that I or any other believer imprisoned with me won't take any oaths because the Bible teaches us not to, rather only say yes or no as it is written, «" But let your 'Yes' be 'Yes,' and your 'No,' 'No.' For whatever is more than these is from the evil one."» Matthew (5: 37)

I started telling them about my life up until the age of 21. How I was a Christian by name only, dead inside and separated from God, practicing all sorts of evils as I was a slave to sin with no way out of the pitiful state I lived. I was without Christ, without hope, as many Christians and non-Christians are around the world today. I told them how I met Jesus personally and came to know Him and how my life completely changed after my salvation.

After they heard my testimony, they didn't have anything to say against me, so they quietly sent me back to my cell.

How I felt during that period?

Here, I would like to add a note for the reader who thinks I had a lion's courage and that I was fearless in all of these situations. Dear reader, that is wrong. I had moments of doubt, fear and anxiety of what awaits me despite my faith that Jesus will save me. Sometimes, I would reach a point of total dread seeing and hearing what merciless torture they would practice on prisoners. Other times, I would feel frustration and despair. But the Lord was with me during it all and sometimes He gave me faith, while at other times; He gave me strength as you will later read. The Bible says, **«"Because of the voice of the enemy, because of the oppression of the wicked; for they bring down trouble upon me, and in wrath they hate me. My heart is severely pained within me, and the terrors of death have fallen upon me; fearfulness and trembling have come upon me, and horror has overwhelmed me. So I said, "Oh, that I had wings like a dove! I would fly away and be at rest. Indeed, I would wander far off, and remain in the wilderness"." » Psalm (55: 3-7)** that is exactly how I felt there.

One day, I asked my cell mates why they were arrested, and as they were explaining why they were in custody, I thought to myself "They all exposed themselves to torture, killing, and execution for trivial crimes and reasons that mean nothing at all." That made me consider myself, "If I die, I will have at least died for something of value." Of course I meant "my faith in Christ", because dying for Christ is gain as the Apostle Paul said, **«"For to me, to live is Christ, and to die is gain."» Philippians (1:21)**

The Dialogue with a Muslim Sheikh, the vision he saw, and how Christ appeared to him personally

One day, I felt a strong longing and nostalgia for the Lord and I didn't have a Bible to read. However, I was full of comforting and consoling verses I had previously learned and kept in my heart for days such as this. I carved the name "**Jesus**" on the cell door using my nails (I had realized the difference between an ordinary door and the door of a prison cell; a door of a prison cell can only be opened from the outside. Someone outside has to open it in order to set the prisoner free. This is exactly the state of a person without Christ, imprisoned inside Satan's cell of sin and destruction, in need of Christ to open his prison door because He is the only one standing outside such a door waiting for us to ask Him and allow Him to set us free). I wrote the name "Jesus" on the door, then, I remembered that He is also God the Savior, so, I wrote the name "**God**" under "Jesus" and the word "**Savior**" under "God", so that the sentence was **"Jesus God the Savior"**. One of the inmates, who was a Muslim leader in the cell and who led them in their daily prayers looked at me and said, "Why did you write Jesus' name first and God's name under it? You shouldn't do that. God's name is greater than Jesus' name." I replied, "I didn't intend to write God's name first, only Jesus' name, then I remembered the phrase "God the

Savior" so I wrote it beneath it." So, he asked me, "Why do you only believe in Jesus? Why don't you believe in our Profit Mohammad and forefathers and Sheikhs?" I answered him, "Jesus has done many miracles in my life in the past, and He still does, and He will do many more in the future. One of them will be setting me free from this prison. So, why must I believe in anyone else? "Another inmate said, "You dream of leaving this prison. No one leaves except as a body inside a box." I said, "Maybe that will be the case for you. You might leave this place as bodies in boxes, but Jesus will set me free." Then I asked everyone listening, "Should I believe in someone who is dead or alive?" and someone quickly and confidently answered, "Of course you should believe in someone alive." So I said, "All the prophets since Abraham until today, including all Christian saints are dead and buried. Jesus is the only one alive!" The Muslim Sheikh friend became furious and said, "You are an unclean pig." I looked at him with a soft smile and did not reply, not out of fear, but out of respect, because he was older than I. I should note that I was the youngest in the cell. One of the inmates said to the Sheikh, "Why do you curse him? He believes that Christ will save him. Let us watch and see if He will." I felt pity for that Sheikh who cursed me and I was sad for his position putting his faith in people and names that he prayed to everyday without avail or answer. Once, he even said, "Is there not one of you that can intercede for us, hear us, or move on behalf of us, you whom I pray to?" Yes, indeed. He said the truth. Because the dead cannot save as it is written: ***"Assemble yourselves and come; draw near together, you who have escaped from the nations. They have no knowledge, who carry the wood of their carved image, <u>and pray to a god that cannot save</u>."*** Isaiah 45: 20. I used to think to myself, "These people are prisoners on the inside as much as they are on the outside. They are spiritual prisoners of sin and flesh prisoners of this jail." As for me, I was aware that I was a prisoner on the outside only, that is my flesh, but free on the inside because Jesus had set me free from my spiritual prison. When I felt love and pity for him, I prayed in my heart, "Lord, you died for them but they reject you with all their power. I have spent many days talking to these people about you and answering all their questions. I will not speak to them any more unless you personally speak to them."

That night, I lied down and slept feeling sad for their states, especially the poor Sheikh, since I really did love him as one who Christ died for. I fell into a deep sleep and when I awoke in the morning I immediately looked at the Sheikh, only to see that he was smiling at me for everybody to see, and he said "Good morning dear" I kindly replied, "Good morning Abu Fulan" (I shall not mention his name for his privacy) The rest of the inmates addressed the Sheikh and said, "Hold on Sheikh, Yesterday you argued with Fadi and cursed him because of his faith in Christ. Today you are saying good morning and greeting him in such a normal attitude as if nothing happened." I arose to wash my face. The Sheikh replied, "No, Fadi will leave this prison. As a Muslim Sheikh I should not repeat what I have seen, but I cannot keep calm. Fadi, come here so I can tell you what happened and what I have seen."

We all sat in a circle, because everyone wanted to hear exactly what happened (keep in mind that the inmates' state of mind in that dark place was devastating and we all wished for any news from anywhere to ease the despair and depression which nearly killed everyone), so the Muslim Sheikh said to me, "Fadi, while you were sleeping, I saw a man in white robe standing near the door you wrote "Jesus" on. A great light emitted from His face, so that I couldn't look at Him. Two men stood by His side, so I felt scared and I thought who could this be? One of the men on His side said to me, "Jesus Christ." (Using his language). Christ then pointed at you, Fadi, while you were asleep and said to me, **"I am responsible for this young man Fadi and I**

will get him out of here. Leave him alone." So I asked Him, "What about me?" (Meaning would He let me out too?). He suddenly disappeared and I awoke in fear. I looked around me and I saw everything just as it was in the vision, even the position of your sleep was the same. I have been waiting for you to wake up since then, which was two hours ago, to tell you that the Christ you believe in will personally set you free from prison. He said so Himself in the vision I saw."

To me, those words that the Lord spoke of me mean a lot. Every believer should put his confidence in those same words and in the full work of Christ for us on the Cross. They mean that the Lord knows me by name, and that he is fully responsible for me, my protection and my salvation, because I am loved and precious to His heart as this is the promise for whoever believes in Him, that He is Lord and God, Savior and Redeemer, *"Fear not, for I have redeemed you; I have called you by your name; you are Mine. When you pass through the waters, I will be with you; and through the rivers, they shall not overflow you. When you walk through the fire, you shall not be burned, nor shall the flame scorch you. For I am the Lord your God, the Holy One of Israel, your Savior; …. Since you were precious in my sight, you have been honored, and I have loved you; therefore I will give men for you, and people for your life." Isaiah (43:1- 3, 4),* and Jesus promised us saying: ***"But the very hairs of your head are all numbered", Mathew 10: 30*** and also said: *«"That you may know that <u>I, the Lord, Who call you by your name</u> … I have even <u>called you by your name</u>; I have named you, though you have not known Me."»* ***Isaiah (45: 3-4).*** For Jesus really knows those who belong to him by name *"...he calls his own sheep by name ..." John 10: 3*

As for the rebuke at the end, it reminds me of the same phrase used in the book of Genesis, *«"..... <u>God has seen my affliction and the labor of my hands, and rebuked you last night."»</u> Genesis (31:42)*

The others gain faith in Christ and change their opinion of Him

When the Sheikh had told his story, I felt amazed and belittled. I felt that I did not deserve this and that it was all above me. I said in my heart, "Who am I that you came in person to speak for me?" I felt tears in my eyes and in my heart I asked, "Lord, will a day really come, when I will be set free and bear witness to everyone of how it came to happen?" I held on to the word of God, *«"I shall not die, but live, and declare the works of the Lord."» Psalm (118:*

17) the rest of the men all said, "Fadi, rejoice, congratulations, Christ personally appeared to declare that He will set you free from prison." My reply was, "You don't believe unless you are rebuked by Christ Himself." They humbly said, "Can Jesus set us free as well?" I answered, "Of course He can. You only have to ask. He is alive."

Some of them received Christ and prayed, "Jesus, save us!" The Sheikh recited a bible verse that I had previously carved on the wall using my nails also, *«"The Lord is my light and my salvation"» Psalm (27:1)* It was truly a day of consolation for all of us. The Sheikh had preached to me personally, and I said to him, "You are lucky. You saw Christ. I am a Christian and I have never seen him in person as you have." However, I believe in Him without seeing and that is far better. *«"Jesus said to him, "Thomas, because you have seen Me, you have believed. Blessed are those who have not seen and yet have believed".»" John (20:29)* Praise God!

The dream of another Muslim cellmate and its interpretation and realization

Two days after that, another inmate in our cell had a dream and told us about it wondering what it could mean? He said, "I dreamed that we were all going out of prison and one person was in charge of releasing us. We stood in a long line, one after the other, and when it was my turn, I saw a tall man, whose face I couldn't see, give me a release document stamped in red. I looked at the red stamp and it was <u>a red cross</u>." I asked them what they thought this dream meant and none of them said a word. Suddenly, the inmate who told us his dream said, "Now I understand what it means. It means that Christ will set us all free from prison when the US forces invade Iraq" It was a strange interpretation for us because that was during the second half of February 2003 and there wasn't a war between Iraq and the US, nor had we heard of any war yet. (Note: Later, I will come back to this man's dream and write about its fulfillment in detail)

My interrogation, the cursing of the word of God, the Bible, mocking it and disregarding it

A few days later, I was called for once more for interrogation and one of the intelligence officers asked me about a verse in the Bible that related to the people of Israel in the Old Testament. He tried to use it as an excuse to accuse Christians of dealing with foreign parties against our country. I answered him, "I don't understand everything that is written in the Bible and in the Old Testament, but you can ask a pastor and he will answer all of your questions. All I know about this verse is that it symbolizes the church (believers in Christ today)". That was according to my simple understanding at the time. So the officer said, "That is nonsense." He meant that the Bible was nonsense. I replied, "It is the Holy Bible." He angrily sent me back to my cell. As I was walking back to my cell with one of the officers, my heart was boiling with rage because of what he had said about the word of God and his disregard of it. It was the only time that I felt anger towards them while I was in prison. I felt jealous for the word of God, a feeling that I hadn't known before. I was raged, and this anger was strange even to me, because I felt that this anger was not merely human or emanating from my being as a person, but it was jealousy for disrespecting the word of God. *"... Behold, the word of the Lord is a reproach to them; they have no delight in it. Therefore I am full of the fury of the Lord. I am weary of holding it in" Jeramiah 6: 10-11,* At that moment, I sensed that if I were to say anything, heaven would have to approve of what I said, *«"Assuredly, I say to you, whatever you bind on earth will be bound in heaven, and whatever you loose on earth will be loosed in heaven."» Matthew (18:18)* I prayed in my heart for the first time something that I wasn't aware of before, "Lord, this government is Earthly, and we are your heavenly government here on Earth, so You choose which one to keep on Earth." I immediately realized that we are not just ordinary believers, but that believers of Christ are God's representatives on Earth, and that violating them means an immediate transgression on the real living God (Christ). When I stepped into my cell, the inmates anxiously asked me, "Fadi, did they beat you? What did they do to you?" I answered angrily, "Those insects they said that the Holy Bible was nonsense. Now hear me well, if this regime lasts for more than two months, then our Christ is false and our Bible is distorted." I did not say that because I literally meant it. I said that because of the intensity and strength of my faith at that moment. I also realized that this government will not stand any longer than two months because it had transgressed against God personally by mocking His word (the Bible) and believers in Christ. I didn't know why I specified a period of two months at the time, as I felt for the first time that any government or kingdom that opposes Christ and the word of God wouldn't survive for long. I spoke words that were more powerful than I was, and I hadn't thought about or considered their consequences, because I could have been executed right then. Everyone viewed me in a strange way after I spoke that way about the fate of the Iraqi government and thought I was spying on them to catch a slip of tongue to prove some accusation against them. Of course I did not mean to say anything personally. Anyway, it is what really happened later on, and it will be the fate and harvest of anyone who sews such seeds in his life. It is also true for individuals and groups too, not just governments. That was the middle of February 2003, *"By the blast of God they perish, And by the breath of His anger they are consumed ... How much more those who dwell in houses of clay, Whose foundation is in the dust, Who are crushed before a moth?", Job 4: 9 and 19,* *"Everyone who falls on that Stone (Jesus) will be broken [in pieces]; but upon whomever It falls, It will crush him [winnow him and scatter him as dust].", Luke 20: 18.*

It's also written: *"How much more those who dwell in houses of clay, whose foundation is in the dust, who are crushed before a moth?" Job 4: 19 ... "He loosens the bonds of kings, and binds their waist with a belt. He leads princes away plundered, and overthrows the mighty", Job 12: 18-19 ... "For God may speak in one way, or in another, yet man does not perceive it. In a dream, in a vision of the night, when deep sleep falls upon men, while slumbering on their beds, then He opens the ears of men, and seals their instruction. In order to turn man from his deed, and conceal pride from man, he keeps back his soul from the Pit, and his life from perishing by the sword.", Job 33: 14-18 ... "He breaks in pieces mighty men without inquiry, and sets others in their place. Therefore He knows their works; He overthrows them in the night, and they are crushed. He strikes them as wicked men in the open sight of others, because they turned back from Him, and would not consider any of His ways, so that they caused the cry of the poor to come to Him; For He hears the cry of the afflicted. When He gives quietness, who then can make trouble? And when He hides His face, who then can see Him, whether it is against a nation or a man alone? - That the hypocrite should not reign, lest the people be ensnared." Job 34: 24-30*

After that, I started explaining to my cellmates that nobody can resist Christ and succeed. I knew that they would be released from prison in the future and that some of them will grow hard-hearted even after that, so I told them Saul's story (who later became a great apostle and witness for Christ) who used to persecute Christians and that he was in charge of killing them, and how Christ appeared to him personally to tell him that it would be difficult for him to resist Christ because it would hurt him in turn. Aggression against Christians is the same as aggression against Christ Himself, and whoever touches them, will be hurt as if touching the eye of God, *«"for he who touches you touches the apple of His eye."» Zechariah (2:8)* and also

«"If God is for us, who can be against us?"» **Romans (8:31)** that is exactly what the Iraqi government had done by opposing believers of Christ and the Bible which ultimately led to its falling. I believe that any Earthly government taking the same path will fall one way or another. It is only a matter of time and we have history to testify to that across the ages. Today the bible is still here; it grows, becomes more powerful and is the bestselling book across the planet in our generation. All of its resistors shall fall one generation at a time, even if they call themselves Christians by name. There are so many Christians today, who resist the bible by their lack of faith in **everything** that is written in it, and by their behaving against its teachings and principles. However, whatever they may say about it, the Bible will always be the living word of God and shall remain forever as Christ said, *«"Heaven and earth will pass away, but My words will by no means pass away."»* **Matthew (24:35)**

When someone rejects Christ and His word, he opens a door for Satan to destroy his life. It is not the loving Christ who destroys human life because He came to save man, not destroy him, *«"The thief (Satan) does not come except to steal, and to kill, and to destroy. I (Jesus) have come that they may have life, and that they may have it more abundantly."» John (10:10)* Continuous rejection of Christ and His word gives official permission for Satan to enter the life of that person or government and steal, kill and destroy him exactly as Christ put it. When man rejects Christ, who *Is* life, there is only the option of death left for him, *«"I call heaven and earth as witnesses today against you, that I have set before you life and death, blessing and cursing; therefore choose life, that both you and your descendants may live; that you may love the Lord your God, that you may obey His voice, and that you may cling to Him, for <u>He is your life</u> and the length of your days; and that you may dwell in the land ...."» Deuteronomy (30: 19-20)* and, *«"Jesus said to him, "I am the way, the truth, and the <u>life</u>. No one comes to the Father except through Me."» John (14:6)*

I may define God's wrath as Him allowing people to sow what they deserve (the fruit of their sins and evil works they did in their lives on Earth) because they rejected what they did not deserve (His free gift of grace presented to them through His son Jesus Christ who died for the forgiveness of their sins and evil works they committed when alive in flesh as well as when they die and leave behind this flesh), *«"So then each of us shall give account of himself to God."» Romans (14:12)* ...*«"For we must all appear before the judgment seat of Christ, that each one may receive the things done in the body, according to what he has done, whether good or bad."» 2 Corinthians (5: 10)*

Meeting the judge to prepare the case and issuance of the final verdict

A few days later, we were called on to meet the High Judge to determine the final verdict in our case. Many put their hope on the mercy of that judge, who I heard was known for being just and doesn't want anyone to be wronged or to admit false confessions because they were beaten by intelligence officers. When my turn came, the judge shouted angrily at me, "What have you people done to this country? Do you want to ruin it? Are you doing all these evils against the government and the country?" I answered, "We haven't done any of that against our country." He replied, "Shut your mouth and don't speak, just sign and certify all these statements and documents filed against you." So I said, "I haven't done any of what is written here against me." He forced me to sign the paper, which unjustly bears false witness against me, and would lead to my execution. He forced me to sign it, in order to raise it to the presidency to get the approval of President Saddam Hussein for my death sentence along with the rest of the innocent faithful brothers who were with me. I was consoled with the word of God, *«"No weapon formed against you shall prosper, and every tongue which rises against you in judgment, you shall condemn."»* **Isaiah (54:17)** I held on to that promise given to me from God and said to the Judge in my heart "We will see who will condemn the other." I was also consoled by *«"The Lord will perfect that which concerns me,"»* **Psalm (138: 8)** I knew in my heart that the Lord would comfort me, rule for me, and defend me in a place called Hakimieh, where there was no one to defend me because lawyers were not allowed. Another verse that comforted me was, *«"If you see the oppression of the poor, and the violent perversion of justice and righteousness in a province, do not marvel at the matter; for high official watches over high official, and higher officials are over them."»* **Ecclesiastes (5:8)** I knew that God's authority was above any Earthly authority, *«"... the Most High God rules in the kingdom of men"»* **Daniel (5:21)** I held fast to those promises because I felt that they were special, alive, and active for me. Thank God because Jesus Christ Himself was the only one defending my case, so that glory is His alone in a place where none of my family, relatives or friends would even know where to look for me. They did not know where I was that whole month in spite doing their best to search for me at police stations and Iraqi security agencies. Indeed, I came to realize that no one can reach me or find out where I was except my dear and faithful friend Jesus as the Bible states that, *«"A man who has friends must himself be friendly, but there is a friend who sticks closer than a brother."»* *Proverbs (18:24)*

«"The Lord will not leave him in his hand, nor condemn him when he is judged."» *Psalm (37:33)*

«"God is our refuge and strength, a very present help in trouble."» *Psalm (46: 1)*

The final verdict from the presidency headquarters issued by Saddam Hussein himself

A few days later, I thought to myself, "Well, if they want to execute us, I should ask for a last request, and it will be to allow me to pray for them." I was sure of where I would be after death, with Christ, because He said, *«"... that where I am, there you may be also."»* *John (14:3)* in my heart, I decided that I would thank them for being the reason for quickly meeting Christ. (I would like to give a message here for every believer that is being oppressed or killed for his faith in Christ: Pray for your enemies and ask God to forgive them before you die (sleep), because they truly do not know what they are doing as the bible says, *«"Then Jesus said, "Father, forgive them, for they do not know what they do".*» *Luke (23:34)* ... «*"And they stoned Stephen as he was calling on God and saying, "Lord Jesus, receive my spirit." Then he knelt down and cried out with a loud voice, "Lord, do not charge them with this sin." And when he had said this, he fell asleep."*» *Acts (7: 59-60)* I almost lost hope of being released from prison, but the Lord daily encouraged me with «*"Wait on the Lord; be of good courage, and He shall strengthen your heart; wait, I say, on the Lord!"*» *Psalm (27:14)* and also with «*"... but God is faithful, who will not allow you to be tempted beyond what you are able, but with the temptation will also make the way of escape, that you may be able to bear it."*» *1Corrintheans (10:13)* I held on to those two promises back then as if they were a living message from the Lord to me. Around two hours after I received these two promises, we were summoned for a final time and the director of intelligence personally read the Presidential decree issued by the presidency on behalf of President Saddam Hussein in which he announced our release from Hakimieh Iraqi intelligence prison. I knew in my heart that Christ was the one who set us free and released us as He said He would, not the government, «*"The king's heart is in the hand of the Lord, like the rivers of water; He turns it wherever He wishes."*» *Proverbs (21:1)* Praise be to Lord Jesus Christ, who commanded the government to do so because His authority is above any other Earthly government. That is how the vision that the Sheikh had seen came to pass, word for word, as we were released on March 1st, 2003 after a full month in prison behind bars. *«"... as the month which was turned from sorrow to joy for them, and from mourning to a holiday"» Esther (9:22)*

«"..The Lord has sent His angel, and has delivered me from the hand of Herod ..."» Acts (12:11)

«"He brought them out of darkness and the shadow of death, and broke their chains in pieces. Oh, that men would give thanks to the Lord for His goodness, and for His wonderful works to the children of men! For He has broken the gates of bronze, and cut the bars of iron in two."» Psalm (107: 14-16)

«"I will go before you and make the crooked places straight; I will break in pieces the gates of bronze and cut the bars of iron."» Isaiah (45:2)

"Who redeems your life from destruction ..." Psalm (103: 4)

"Who delivered us from so great a death, and does deliver us; in whom we trust that He will still deliver us", (2nd Corinthians 1: 10)

Notice: God had given me a stock of His word before I entered this trial and that helped me stand firm despite the fear and death that surrounded me. It is important for every believer to stock up on God's word and continuously read it, because it will be very useful in times of trial and turn into living, divine commands which will save in times of distress and deliver from death as the Bible declares in *Hebrews (11:33)*, *«"who through faith subdued kingdoms, worked righteousness, obtained promises, stopped the mouths of lions, quenched the violence of fire, escaped the edge of the sword, out of weakness were made strong,"»*

Continuously reading the Bible is very necessary, because the information will turn into declarations under different circumstances when the Holy Ghost transforms that information inside you at a certain time into a direct announcement from God, and when you speak them with your tongue and lips, they come to pass. We all pray that the will of God is done on Earth as it is in heaven, but we forget that the things of heaven are all in the Bible, and whoever wants to know the will of God in heaven only has to read the Holy Bible. Then, when he speaks the word, he declares that what is in heaven must happen on Earth, and only then does the will of God come to pass.

Our release followed by being secretly pursued and spied on

This situation reminds me of when Pharaoh set the people of God free, but he continued to chase them, pursue them and spy on them.

«*"The enemy said, 'I will pursue, I will overtake, I will divide the spoil; my desire shall be satisfied on them. I will draw my sword, my hand shall destroy them.' You blew with Your wind, the sea covered them; they sank like lead in the mighty waters. "Who is like You, Lord, among the gods? Who is like You, glorious in holiness, fearful in praises, doing wonders? You stretched out Your right hand; the earth swallowed them. You in Your mercy have led forth the people whom You have redeemed; You have guided them in Your strength to Your holy habitation. "The people will hear and be afraid;"*»
Exodus (15: 9-14)

«*"Be merciful to me, O God, for man would swallow me up; fighting all day he oppresses me. My enemies would hound me all day, for there are many who fight against me, O Most High. Whenever I am afraid, I will trust in You. In God (I will praise His word), in God I have put my trust; I will not fear. What can flesh do to me? All day they twist my words; all their thoughts are against me for evil. They gather together, they hide; they mark my steps, when they lie in wait for my life. Shall they escape by iniquity? In anger cast down the peoples, O God!"»* Psalm (56:1-7)

The driver, who had previously driven insanely fast, let us in the car and then dropped us off in a public place in Baghdad after the intelligence officer apologized for what happened to us *"So they came and apologized to them. After they escorted them out ..." Acts 16: 39 TLV*, He had asked me before we left the prison building, "Why are you here?" I replied, "You are the government. You should tell us why you brought us here." We were released but under observation and they had banned us from gathering in houses for prayer. They were pursuing us and spying on us after we were released, and they did their best to prevent us from talking with others till their judgment came to pass as it is written they were *"forbidding us to speak to the Gentiles that they may be saved, so as always to fill up the measure of their sins; but wrath has come upon them to the uttermost.", 1ˢᵗ Thessalonians 2: 16*, and the prayer meetings that they were trying to stop with all their might, was the only thing that would save them from the perdition that was going to befall the country and they were unaware of it. If they had allowed us to pray for them, the country today would have been in a better state because the Lord has commanded us to pray for rulers and all those who are in authority. However, what can we do if the officials in charge of protecting the country were willfully refusing and resisting protection? *In 1 Timothy (2: 1-4), Paul says, «You therefore, my son, be strong in the grace that is in Christ Jesus. And the things that you have heard from me among many witnesses, commit these to faithful men who will be able to teach others also. You therefore must endure hardship as a good soldier of Jesus Christ. No one engaged in warfare entangles himself with the affairs of this life, that he may please him who enlisted him as a soldier."»*

Praising and thanking God frees and releases from captivity

During one of my last few days in prison, I was looking at the door of the prison and remembered the English praise song by **Don Moen** that says,

"God will make a way

Where there seems to be no way

He works in ways we cannot see

He will make a way for me …"

My hope was in God and His salvation for me, because *«"Surely His salvation is near to those who fear Him"»* *Psalm (85: 9)* The last thing I did a few moments before I left prison, was thank The Lord with all my heart for this trial. I was summoned and released afterwards along with the brethren who were with me.

Praising God truly did open the gates of the prison *«"But at midnight Paul and Silas were praying and singing hymns to God, and the prisoners were listening to them. Suddenly there was a great earthquake, so that the foundations of the prison were shaken; and immediately all the doors were opened and everyone's chains were loosed."» Acts (16: 25-26)*

I encourage you to put your faith, hope and dependency on God alone with no other, for *«" Cursed is the man who trusts in man and makes flesh his strength, whose heart departs from the Lord"» Jeremiah (17: 5)* rather, *«"Blessed is the man who trusts in the Lord, And whose hope is the Lord."» Jeremiah (17: 7)*

The beginning of the war in Iraq and the falling of the government as the events were coming to pass

Jesus said to whoever heard of Him or His word, *«"… But everyone who <u>hears</u> these sayings of Mine, and <u>does not do</u> them, will be like a foolish man who built his house on the sand: and the rain descended, the floods came, and the winds blew and beat on that house; and it fell. <u>And great was its fall.</u>"» Matthew (7: 26-27)*

This principle applies to presidents, governments and countries, groups and individuals and every human being on the face of the planet, even if they aren't Christian and do not believe in the Bible.

Less than three weeks later, the war on Iraq began. The Iraqi government fell in less than three weeks, and I saw with my own eyes lions turning into rats without a place to shelter them and what was written had happened, *«"Only with your eyes shall you look, and see the reward of the wicked."» Psalm (91:8)*

«"I have seen the wicked in great power, and spreading himself like a native green tree. Yet he passed away, and behold, he was no more; indeed I sought him, but he could not be found."» Psalm (37: 35-36)

«"There they are in great fear where no fear was, for God has scattered the bones of him who encamps against you; you have put them to shame, because God has despised them."»
Psalm (53:5)

«"since it is a righteous thing with God to repay with tribulation those who trouble you"» 2 Thessalonians (1: 6)

«"For evildoers shall be cut off; But those who wait on the Lord, They shall inherit the earth. For yet a little while and the wicked shall be no more; Indeed, you will look carefully for his place, But it shall be no more. But the meek shall inherit the earth, And shall delight themselves in the abundance of peace.
The wicked plots against the just, And gnashes at him with his teeth. The Lord laughs at him, For He sees that his day is coming. The wicked have drawn the sword And have bent their bow, To cast down the poor and needy, To slay those who are of upright conduct. Their sword shall enter their own heart, And their bows shall be broken."» Psalm (37: 9- 15)

«" Wait on the Lord, And keep His way, And He shall exalt you to inherit the land; When the wicked are cut off, you shall see it."» Psalm (37: 34)

«" For He has delivered me out of all trouble; And my eye has seen its desire upon my enemies."» Psalm (54: 7)

I would like to advise anyone in a post, the president of any nation or government that Jesus is looking for you, He loves you, and He died on the cross for you to redeem you of your sins and their punishment which is damnation on Earth and then the ever after. Open your heart to Him, and allow Him to forgive your sins, which you try to ignore every time you feel guilty by doing some good works that you think are good, when in reality they are useless, as the Bible declares, *«"But we are all like an unclean thing, and all our righteousnesses are like filthy rags;"» Isaiah (64:6)* The only cure for your guilt and condemnation is placing your faith in what Christ has done for you and not the good works that you try to do to cure your guilt and sin. Jesus fully paid the price for your sins on the cross, and all you have to do is believe in what he has done for you, open your heart to Him, and not reject His love and free forgiveness of your sins today.

A few days after the government fell, I remembered the dream that one my inmates told in the cell; that Christ would free them through the US forces. So, I took one of my friends with me and we went to ask for him, as I knew he was a carpenter in a hospital when we were in prison. We went to that hospital and I asked for him and he wasn't there at the time, but, one of his friends said, "What do you want with Abu Fulan" (I don't want to mention his name for the sake of his privacy). I explained that we were cell mates, because his friend was afraid to tell me anything about him since the people still feared the recently fallen Iraqi government. He took me aside and said, "Abu Fulan has been released by the US forces that came to Abu Ghraib prison and set everyone free because they had been moved there during the war, probably because they feared that Hakimieh intelligence prison would be bombarded again like in 1991." That is what we were told while we were in prison. Praise the living Christ who showed this inmate the dream and its interpretation, glory be to His name.

The vision that my mother had seen while we were arrested

My mother had witnessed our arrest along with a large number of believers who were there for the worship service in that hall. When they arrested us few men, my mother was scared and attempted to rescue me from them asking, "Who are you? Why are you arresting my son?" All they said was that they were going to bring us back home in a couple of hours. My mother fainted and almost fell to the ground when some brothers and sisters helped her and took her to a nearby hospital. While she was unconscious she saw a vision which she later told me about when I was released from prison.

"While I was unconscious, I saw in a vision, part of heaven that was incredibly beautiful that it's difficult to describe. It was the most magnificent place I had ever seen. At that moment I heard a voice in my mind that said, "Fadi is on a mission."

That vision gave my mother courage and comfort while she was in that state. My mother awoke in a car on the way to the hospital and she said to the brothers who were taking her, "Fadi is on a mission!" She spoke with a tone full of hope that I was on a mission from the Lord and that I would come back. The brothers thought that she was hallucinating.

It was truly an encouraging vision from God the day we were arrested because I was really on a mission inside that place and the Lord let me out when I was done. My mission, dear reader, also includes writing this for you to read and to be encouraged because Jesus is alive and He is the same yesterday, today and forever. All glory, honor, and worship is His forever, Amen.

An important notice: Judgment and condemnation come to countries, states, individuals and groups because of their rejection of the salvation of Jesus for

them and the word of God, and any state that fights the gospel, even if it was one day based on the Bible (like the United States of America), it will be doomed to perdition one way or another. This applies to everyone, therefore, it is an opportunity today for any state and its people to be saved, regardless of its deteriorating condition, if it accepts God's gift of salvation and eternal life. «"For God so loved the world that He gave His only begotten Son, that whoever believes in Him should not perish but have everlasting life. For God did not send His Son into the world to condemn the world, but that the world through Him might be saved."» John (3:16-17)

A missile flies above me and words of judgment announced over the country:

One day, during the war between the US and Iraq, I was standing in what was our home's yard watching as some very nearby missiles were passing right above me. I believe they were called Tomahawk Missiles. They were headed towards the Iraqi Intelligence Building, which I lived nearby, to destroy it. They were so close, that I could actually read a few English letters on it and see their white color with flame coming out of it despite the darkness. A voice inside said, "This is the judgment!"

Yes, dear reader, hearing those words was not a coincidence. It was the season of judgment for Iraq for the aversion that the Iraqi government had towards the Lord who redeemed them and died for them on the cross, for their disbelief and their resistance of Him and His holy word. This judgment was "reaping what we deserve (the seeds of our evil works) because we rejected what we are not worthy of (Jesus – who, in His death, resurrection, and living presence among us today, took our sin and its consequences on the cross."

«*"He brings the princes to nothing; He makes the judges of the earth useless. Scarcely shall they be planted, Scarcely shall they be sown, Scarcely shall their stock take root in the earth, When He will also blow on them, And they will wither, And the whirlwind will take them away like stubble."*»
Isaiah (40: 23-24)

«*"He destroyed the firstborn of Egypt, Both of man and beast.*
[9] He sent signs and wonders into the midst of you, O Egypt, Upon Pharaoh and all his servants. He defeated many nations And slew mighty kings— Sihon king of the Amorites, Og

king of Bashan, And all the kingdoms of Canaan"»
Psalm (135: 8-11)

An important Note:

Whoever persecutes a true believer in Jesus, is in fact persecuting Jesus Himself, and as a result, the persecutor is harming himself just as Saul did before he personally met Jesus Christ. *«"And when we all had fallen to the ground, I heard a voice speaking to me and saying in the Hebrew language, 'Saul, Saul, why are you persecuting Me? It is hard for you to kick against the goads.'"» Acts (26: 14)*
«"Then Saul, still breathing threats and murder against the disciples of the Lord, went to the high priest and asked letters from him to the synagogues of Damascus, so that if he found any who were of the Way, whether men or women, he might bring them bound to Jerusalem. As he journeyed he came near Damascus, and suddenly a light shone around him from heaven. Then he fell to the ground, and heard a voice saying to him, "Saul, Saul, why are you persecuting Me?" And he said, "Who are You, Lord?" Then the Lord said, "I am Jesus, whom you are persecuting.¹ It is hard for you to kick against the goads." So he, trembling and astonished, said, "Lord, what do You want me to do?" Then the Lord said to

him, "Arise and go into the city, and you will be told what you must do."» Acts (9: 1-6)

Saul was not persecuting against Jesus personally in the flesh as he had never seen Him before, rather he was persecuting against Jesus' disciples and followers. Jesus confronted him and said, «"Why do you persecute me? … I am Jesus who you persecute against."»

Abusing those who are Christ's is like abusing Jesus Christ personally, and all you have to do is watch and see the consequences.

What is the worst decision any government can make?
I have never experienced a worse moment, which can only show that the Iraqi government's evil had come to its fullness and that its end was near due to its lack of knowledge. How do they dare raid and the house of the King of kings and arrest His body of believers while they are gathered in His name, and think that you will get away with it. A decision you should have thought a through a thousand times before you make! Look at how Iraq was inevitably invaded and all the destruction they brought to themselves and their country. The word says to believers in Christ, His body, *«"For no one ever hated his own flesh,*

but nourishes and cherishes it, just as the Lord does the church"» Ephesians (5: 29) «" And He put all things under His feet, and gave Him to be head over all things to the church, which is His body, the fullness of Him who fills all in all."» Ephesians (1: 22-23) and Jesus said, *«"For where two or three are gathered together in My name, I am there in the midst of them."» Matthew (18: 20)*

Yes, (Jesus was in our midst while we gathered in His name!) If someone had broken into my home and assaulted my family members in front of me, I assure you dear reader, I will not let him get away with it and leave peacefully no matter how kind , loving and peaceful I am. More so, the Iraqi intelligence raided a place where Jesus' family had gathered in His name and did not even think that the King of kings and Lord of lords was in the midst watching over everything. Look at the destruction and perish it led our dear country to later. This wasn't the first time that a government caused the damage and destruction of its country by violating God's people. In **Exodus 7- 14,** we read of how pharos's resistance to the Lord and His word that He would send through His official spokesperson, Moses the prophet, led to the destruction of his land and the perish of his people, who suffered the consequences of his decisions against God. The people were groaning because of the resistance of their leader to the word of God and His prophet Moses as they suffered from 10 severe strikes that were either economic strikes, which harmed the country's economy leading to several losses from lack of water, the death of fish and livestock to harmful insects, or diseases that struck the people and the animals, in addition to natural strikes that came in the form of climate change and the agitation of nature, which affected all agricultural products, not to mention locust that destroyed the crops blowing away the economy. The people also suffered from darkness that prevailed in the land, which is currently depicted in power outages. There was also the strike of death which the leader's household personally suffered from along with his people, for resisting God, when his first born son died with every other first born son n the country. Finally, the cruelty of his heart towards God and His word, led to his and his army's death making God's word in *Proverbs (29: 2)* fully applicable «*"When the righteous are in authority, the people rejoice; But when a wicked man rules, the people groan."*» Today, how many evil rulers are in high ranking positions and causing the ruin of themselves and others around them by making decisions that are rooted in corrupted profane minds not in the word of God. The result is their destruction along with their countries and people without realizing why. I give them the reason here, in these few lines along with the solution. Dear reader, the reason for the ruin of countries, governments and people is written in *Jeremiah (9: 12-4)* «*"The plunderers have come On all the desolate heights in the wilderness, For the sword of the Lord shall devour From one end of the land to the other end of the land; No flesh shall have peace. They have sown wheat but reaped thorns; They have put themselves to pain but do not profit. But be ashamed of your harvest Because of the fierce anger of the Lord." Thus says the Lord: "Against all My evil neighbors who touch the inheritance which I have caused My people Israel to inherit—behold, I will pluck them out of their land and pluck out the house of Judah from among them."*»

<u>We, as a people, should have good awareness and distinction in our presidential elections in order to choose those who are righteous, and who respect and honor the word of God, the Bible, to be in high presidential and government positions for the good of the country and the good of the people lest we are ruled by wicked rulers only to groan and hide out of their fault. It is written, «*"When the wicked arise, men hide themselves; But when they perish, the righteous increase."*» *Proverbs (28: 28)*</u>

Some might think I rejoiced when the Iraqi government fell, and rejoiced when President Saddam Hussein fell because they persecuted and mistreated me as well as the rest of the faithful brothers for no reason. If that's what you think, dear reader, allow me to tell you that you are wrong. I am not and will not rejoice in the fall of whoever disagrees with me in ideology or faith in Christ and the word of God, because eventually he will only hurt himself. The day President Saddam Hussein fell in the hands of US forces, I watched that scene on television and felt sad for only one reason, that "God is not happy when a sinful man dies, rather He is happy when that person repents and runs back to Him." As the bible puts it, *«"I say to you that likewise there will be more joy in heaven over one sinner who repents … I say to you, there is joy in the presence of the angels of God over one sinner who repents."»* Luke *(15:7 &10)* This is the God that I came to know in the bible and who I learned about from His word, Who also said, *«"…says the Lord God, 'I have no pleasure in the death of the wicked, but that the wicked turn from his way and live."»* Ezekiel *(33:11*) and in *Proverbs (24:17)* *«"Do not rejoice when your enemy falls, and do not let your heart be glad when he stumbles"»* and in *1 Timothy (2: 3-4)* *«"who (God) desires all men to be saved and to come to the knowledge of the truth."»* Christ also taught us to love our enemies, bless those who curse us and pray for whoever oppresses us, *«"You have heard that it was said, 'You shall love your neighbor and hate your enemy.' But I say to you, love your enemies, bless those who curse you, do good to those who hate you, and pray for those who spitefully use you and persecute you, that you may be sons of your Father in heaven; for He makes His sun rise on the evil and on the good, and sends rain on the just and on the unjust."» Matthew (5:43-45)* I had been praying for them indeed. It is not a pleasant thing for man to spend his eternity in hell when he has a chance here on Earth to choose to live with God forever through faith in what Christ has done for him on the cross.

It is personally painful for God more than it is for us believers, because once, we too were enemies of Christ like the rest of people, although we had the "Christians" title and used to go to meetings at church or exercise some religious practices which don't hold any value whatsoever, in comparison with what Christ did for us; reconciliation with God the father in His death on the cross. *«"Now all things are of God, who has reconciled us to Himself through Jesus Christ, and has given us the ministry of reconciliation, that is, that God was in Christ reconciling the world to Himself, not imputing their trespasses to them"» 2 Corinthians (5: 18-19)* God the father loves everyone without prejudice, Christians or non-Christians, Buddhists or communists, and even those who resist Him. We were all, without exception, enemies of God, but He redeemed us for free with His grace as the Bible says, *«"for **all** have sinned and fall short of the glory of God, being justified freely by His grace through the redemption that is in Christ Jesus, whom God set forth as a propitiation by His blood, through faith, to demonstrate His righteousness, because in His forbearance God had passed over the sins that were previously committed"» Romans (3: 23-25)* He wants salvation for all through faith in what Jesus Christ did for them on the cross, His death and resurrection from the dead as the Bible declares, *«"For God so loved the world that He gave His only begotten Son, that whoever believes in Him should not perish but have everlasting life. For God did not send His Son into the world to condemn the world, but that the world through Him might be saved. He who believes in Him is not condemned; but he who does not believe is condemned already, because he has not believed in the name of the only begotten Son of God."» John (3: 16-18)* He is alive today for anyone who asks for Him. God is not happy when people who don't believe in Him today die, and He hurts for every soul that doesn't believe in Him because it will be doomed although it had a chance to be saved, that chance is available **now**, *«"Therefore, as the Holy Spirit says: "Today, if you will hear His voice, do not harden your hearts"»* Hebrew (3: 7 -8)* In the meantime, Satan is increasing ferocity and cruelty to mislead, dismantle and destroy their lives, because he knows that his eternal destiny is inevitably doom.

God has no favoritism among humans, and does not differentiate between people. Everyone will reap what they sow here on Earth and in eternity. *«"tribulation and anguish, on every soul of man who does evil, of the Jew first and also of the Greek; but glory, honor, and peace to everyone who works what is good, to the Jew first and also to the Greek. For there is no partiality with God."»* Romans (2: 9-11)*

Jesus our defender

Jesus Christ was, still is, and always will be alive. He still speaks through His word, the Bible and through visions and dreams, as well as events. He still defends His people who believe in His name. All we have to do is believe and hold on to Him and His word, and not harden our hearts because He loves us and died for us. I recently learned to rely only on what Jesus did for me on the cross and nothing else. I used to wrongfully think that I could do something for the

Lord or add something to what He has done for me, but I would stumble and fall every time, rather I would sin more when I tried to rely on myself and my way of thinking and performance to gain the satisfaction of God even after I accepted faith in Him. It was because of my lack of knowledge in God's word and God's nature. I used to sometimes think that He had abandoned me because I had abandoned Him, or that He would act the way I did with Him, or that when I sinned against Him or stumbled and fell that He would leave me, but I was wrong. It is as someone once said, "Religiosity is a human attempt to reach God (through the works and mentality of performance), but real Christian life is actually God attempting to reach us (through a full work done by Jesus on the cross for us" because He is not a human like us, He is also God, *«"Therefore, in all things He had to be made like His brethren, that He might be a merciful and faithful High Priest in things pertaining to God, to make propitiation for the sins of the people. For in that He Himself has suffered, being tempted, He is able to aid those who are tempted."» Hebrews (2: 17-18)*

There is nothing that pleases the Lord, but faith in what Jesus did for us on the cross. His work is whole and doesn't lack anything. All we have to do is have confidence in His complete work not our works, whether they are good or evil. The Bible declares, *«"But without faith it is impossible to please Him, for he who comes to God must believe that He is and that He is rewards those who diligently seek Him."» Hebrew (11: 6)* if we want to do God's will, we only have to believe in Jesus and rely on Him and His full work for us. *«"Then they said to Him, "What shall we do, that we may work the works of God?" Jesus answered and said to them, "This is the work of God; that you believe in Him whom He sent"."» John (6: 28-29)*

A prayer for salvation

Dear reader,

God is searching for you to find you. You may think that you are looking for Him, but He wants you to experience the fullness of eternal life with Him while you are still here on Earth, through faith in what Jesus has done on the cross for you. He gave up His life so you could have His. Jesus, the son of God, became a man, so you could become a son of God. He wants you to have everything and He wants to provide all your needs according to His glorious riches in Christ Jesus as He promised, *«"And my God shall supply all your need according to His riches in glory by Christ Jesus."» Philippians (4:19)* So, please pray this prayer if you would like to experience protection, deliverance, forgiveness, love, faithfulness, provision, and reconciliation and much more as I have with Christ and that which I still do to this day.

Say this prayer out loud admitting it with your mouth and trust that you will not be disappointed, «*"that if you confess with your mouth the Lord Jesus and believe in your heart that God has raised Him from the dead, you will be saved. For with the heart one believes unto righteousness, and with the mouth confession is made unto salvation. For the Scripture says, "Whoever believes on Him will not be put to shame"."*»

Pray this: **"Lord Jesus Christ, I know that You are alive and that You exist. I ask that You forgive my sins and cleanse me of them all with Your holy blood that was shed on the cross for me. I thank You for Your death and resurrection for me, and I ask You to enter my heart and my life now to give me eternal life and to write my name in the book of life. I thank You because You have heard me and answered my prayer. I thank You because You have chosen me to believe in You before the founding of Earth. Amen."**

Jesus said, *«"All that the Father gives Me will come to Me, and the one who comes to Me I will by no means cast out."» John (6: 37)*

You are now a son of God as Christ promised ...

If you prayed this prayer with all your heart, you have become a son of God through faith in Christ who gave you that authority. Welcome to the family of the real, creator of heaven and Earth, living God. He declared, *«"But as many as received Him, to them He gave the right to become children of God, to those who believe in His name: who were born, not of blood, nor of the will of the flesh, nor of the will of man, but of God."» John (1: 12-13)*

Now prepare yourself for the journey that Jesus will lead you through for the rest of your days here. It is a journey punctuated by pain and discomfort, distress and comfort, doubt and faith, fear and force, need and provision. You might stumble and fall from time to time but He will redeem you because He is faithful and living. Jesus is alive and He has promised that He will not forsake you or leave you. He will not give up even when you stumble, fall and sin, because He is forever unchanging despite the change in us. Do not lose hope if you cannot please Him, because all you have to do is trust that He has already satisfied God the father for you in every way. Trust Him because He is unchanging. Don't trust in yourself because you do change and He will form you and change you to become more like Him in everything. *«"For whom He foreknew, He also predestined to be conformed to the image of His Son, that He might be the firstborn among many brethren."»* *Romans (8: 29)* It's an ongoing process as long as you live. Jesus is the eldest brother and you will experience the power of His real and sincere brotherhood. He will remain with you forever because of the covenant between you and Him made with His own blood that He shed on the cross for you, not because of a covenant or a promise that you have made or because of what you have done or what you're doing now or what you will do in the future, whether it is good or evil. Thank God for His rich grace. Always trust in it and in the Bible looking towards Jesus, not yourself or others, lest your strength faint. *«"Looking unto Jesus, the author and finisher of our faith, who for the joy that was set before Him endured the cross, despising the shame, and has sat down at the right hand of the throne of God. For consider Him who endured such hostility from sinners against Himself, lest you become weary and discouraged in your souls."»* *Hebrews (12: 2-3)* and He will always keep you, *«"Now to Him who is able to keep you from stumbling, and to present you faultless before the presence of His glory with exceeding joy, to God our Savior, who alone is wise, be glory and majesty, dominion and power, both now and forever. Amen."»* Jude (1: 24-25)

"For it was fitting for Him, for whom are all things and by whom are all things, in bringing many sons to glory, to make the captain of their salvation perfect through sufferings. For both He who sanctifies and those who are being sanctified are all of one, for which reason He is not ashamed to call them brethren"» Hebrews (2: 10-11)

«"Teaching them to observe all things that I have commanded you; and lo, I am with you always, even to the end of the age. Amen."» Matthew (28:20)

«"Why do the nations rage, and the people plot a vain thing? The kings of the earth set themselves, and the rulers take counsel together, against the Lord and against His Anointed, saying, "Let us break Their bonds in pieces And cast away Their cords from us." He who sits in the heavens shall laugh; the Lord shall hold them in derision. Then He shall speak to them in His wrath, and distress them in His deep displeasure: "Yet I have set My King On My holy hill of Zion." "I will declare the decree:

the Lord has said to Me, 'You are My Son, today I have begotten You. Ask of Me, and I will give You the nations for Your inheritance, and the ends of the earth for Your possession. You shall break them with a rod of iron; You shall dash them to pieces like a potter's vessel.'" Now therefore, be wise, O kings; be instructed, you judges of the earth. Serve the Lord with fear, and rejoice with trembling. <u>Kiss the Son, lest He be angry, and you perish in the way</u>, when His wrath is kindled but a little. Blessed are all those who put their trust in Him."» **Psalm (2: 1-12)**

The coming of Christ to reign on Earth is near. Be ready to meet the Beloved who will judge the Earth... always stand firm in God's word, the Bible.

«"Your right hand shall teach You awesome things. Your arrows are sharp in the heart of the King's enemies; the peoples fall under You. Your throne, O God, is forever and ever; a scepter of righteousness is the scepter of Your kingdom."» Psalm (45: 4-6)

«"So that men will say, "Surely there is a reward for the righteous; surely He is God who judges in the earth"."» *Psalm (58:11)*

«"Do not put your trust in princes, nor in a son of man, in whom there is no help. His spirit departs, he returns to his earth; in that very day his plans perish. Happy is he who has the God of Jacob for his help, whose hope is in the Lord his God, who made heaven and earth, the sea, and all that is in them; who keeps truth forever, who executes justice for the oppressed, who gives food to the hungry. The Lord gives freedom to the <u>prisoners</u>. The Lord opens the eyes of the blind; the Lord raises those who are bowed down; the Lord loves the righteous. The Lord watches over the strangers; He relieves the fatherless and widow; but the way of <u>the wicked He turns upside down.</u>"» Psalm (146: 3-9)

«"Give us help from trouble, for the help of man is useless."» Psalm (60: 11)

The proverb of the garbage collector and the intelligence officer

A lesson about the spiritual authority of a believer

«"Then the seventy returned with joy, saying, "Lord, even the demons are subject to us in Your name." And He said to them, "I saw Satan fall like lightning from heaven. Behold, I give you the authority to trample on serpents and scorpions, and over all the power of the enemy, and nothing shall by any means hurt you. Nevertheless do not rejoice in this, that the spirits are subject to you, but rather rejoice because your names are written in heaven".» Luke (10: 17-20)

One day, while I was in my cell in prison, something strange happened. I heard the voices of a few men talking loudly in their cells. A voice inside said, "Listen." So, I started attentively listening to the conversation that was going on. One of the prisoners begged to have only one cigarette to smoke (of course he knew that it wasn't allowed during his imprisonment in Hakimieh Intelligence Prison even if he was addicted) from one of the officers as he was probably addicted and couldn't tolerate it any longer. However, the strange thing was that the officer was trembling and stuttering when he answered him in the middle of the night, and it seemed that there was no one in charge except for him on our floor. He asked the prisoner from outside the cell, "Who is that? What do you want?" It appeared as if the officer was scared although he had authority over all the prisoners, around 100 of them, in well-locked cells on that floor. When the rest of the inmates heard the conversation between the prisoner, who was behind bars, and the scared officer, they too started shouting at the officer and banging the doors as they could sense his fear.

A few days later, a garbage collector came early morning and shouted in the hallways for all the prisoners to hear, "Prisoners, prepare the garbage!" He shouted with authority as if he was the intelligence director. All the inmates feared him, especially the inmates in my cell. The Sheikh quickly got up with the garbage bag in his hand and stood by the small opening in the door waiting for the collector to come take the bag. When the garbage collector reached our cell, he shouted with great authority, "Get your garbage ready you here!" and when he opened the small opening, it turned out he was a short young man who couldn't be more than 20 years old in comparison with the inmates. Any prisoner could merely scream at him to knock him down according to the norms and standards of physics and age. But there was something different about this garbage collector; it was that he knew the authority and power of the place where he works. He knew that the authority was given to him by senior officials in the Hakimieh intelligence. It appears that he did not consider himself, his young age, or his size and job, which is considered the lowest job in Iraq and in the governance of the intelligence, rather he was saturated in knowing who he was, where he works and the authority given to him, and he was acted accordingly in spite of being a garbage collector. When he acted and behaved according to that authority, he forced all the prisoners submit to him in fear.

That position gave me insight into something very important. The officer didn't realize the authority or the power that was given to him over the prisoners as an intelligence officer which is considered a high rank in that building. He was looking at himself and his fear instead of using his authority to silence and submit those prisoners. When he failed to use the authority that was given to him by the government, the prisoners insulted and sneered at him. I learned an important lesson for my life and the lives of believers in Christ who have been given authority by Him and don't use it against all Satan's evil powers. Then, all imprisoned evil spirits who have been disarmed of any power will attack them and overcome them with their lies. This is the case with many of the believers in Christ today. It seems that the garbage collector realized the authority that was given to him better than the intelligence officer, despite the fact that the garbage collector holds a minimum function in the governance of the intelligence building and the lowest job in the country. But he acted on his authority not considering himself, his limitations or his job.

Today, as believers in Christ, we have been given full authority by Him, *«"And Jesus came and spoke to them, saying, "All authority has been given to Me in heaven and on earth. Go therefore and make disciples of all the nations, baptizing them in the name of the Father and of the Son and of the Holy Spirit, teaching them to observe all things that I have commanded you; and lo, I am with you always, even to the end of the age." Amen."»* Matthew (28: 18-20) ... *«"He who hears you hears Me, he who rejects you rejects Me, and he who rejects Me rejects Him who sent Me." Then the seventy returned with joy, saying, "Lord, even the demons are subject to us in Your name." And He said to them, "I saw Satan fall like lightning from heaven. Behold, <u>I give you the authority</u> to trample on serpents and scorpions, and over all the power of the enemy, and nothing shall by any means hurt you. Nevertheless do not rejoice in this, that* *the spirits are subject to you, but rather rejoice because your names are written in heaven".* "» *Luke (10: 16-20)* we should walk in that authority to submit all the power of Satan under us. The devil and all of his helpers know well that they are prisoners without power or ability over us, unless we allow them. We must never give Satan place to prey on us with his lies, *«"nor give place to the devil." Ephesians (4:27)* we all fall into these traps every now and then, but it is time to realize righteousness, *«"Awake to righteousness, and do not sin; for some do not have the knowledge of God."» 1 Corinthians (15:34)*

My prayer for every real believer and soldier of Christ is that you don't rely on yourself but in the full work of Christ on the cross, and that you may have a mentality that understands your authority as the garbage collector did, and that you continuously walk in the authority given to you by Christ.

All glory, honor, worship is our Lord's forever and ever. Amen.

How should we love one another as believers in Christ?
One day, while I was still in prison, I was handcuffed and led to a long pathway that held several investigation rooms on both the right and left sides. They sat me down on the floor in front of one of those torture rooms to wait my turn for investigation, so I heard one of the Iraqi intelligence officers probing someone inside the room I would enter when they were done. They were cruelly beating him, hitting him with violence I had never imagined or heard of while he was uselessly screaming for help. When they brought him out I found out that he was denying being the brother of one of the men waiting his turn for investigation next to me. They asked him, "Do you know this person?" (Referring to his brother), he answered, "No, I don't know him at all." At the same time his brother was saying, "I am your brother so why do you deny it?" and he would reply, "Who are you? I don't know you." This beaten man was absolutely denying that this man was his brother because apparently if he admitted being his brother his fate would definitely be merciless perdition considering the crimes they had committed at the time. Then, they brought him back in again and beat him with iron chairs and hard tools that I could hear his bones being crushed until his voice dropped and he lost consciousness. They summoned a doctor just to see whether he had died or if he was still

alive, and I heard the doctor say to them, " If you continue to beat him this way he will die so they gave him a rest, and when he awoke they proceeded to beat him and torture him again. I heard that going on for about two hours as I was sitting there on the floor waiting my turn to enter that room, but thanks be to God who saved me again that day from them and I was sent to my cell without investigation because I asked the Lord for help as I almost had a psychiatric break-down from what I heard and saw, if it wasn't for the grace of God that raised me up strongly that day. **The lesson I want to address here is brotherly love that should be practiced among true believers of Jesus Christ.** Later one day, the intelligence officers brought me into one of these investigation rooms and asked me if I knew a specific person who was in fact a brother in Christ and servant of the Lord Jesus. However, he was a foreigner and they expected me to deny knowing him because that would save my life and might not be tortured that day. My answer seemed to surprise them, "of course I know him, he is like a brother to me, and he used to eat, drink and even sometimes sleep in our home as one of our brothers." They didn't expect such an answer; rather they expected me to deny that I knew him as everyone does in times of adversity. When they heard a truthful answer, they relaxed and started speaking calmly after they had been getting ready to torture me.

Here I would like to add the following: Our love for one another as believers in Christ should be as strong as death as the bible declares, and not just when circumstances are good and comfortable, «*"And above all things have fervent love for one another, for "love will cover a multitude of sins".*"»*1 Peter (4:8)* We must also learn that we are dealing with Christ Himself when we are dealing with each other, «*"He who receives you receives Me, and he who receives Me receives Him who sent Me. He who receives a prophet in the name of a prophet shall receive a prophet's reward. And he who receives a righteous man in the name of a righteous man shall receive a righteous man's reward. And whoever gives one of these little ones only a cup of cold water in the name of a disciple, assuredly, I say to you, he shall by no means lose his reward."*» *Matthew (10: 40-42)* Yes, we should always welcome each other and love one another as such, «*"Set me as a seal upon your heart, as a seal upon your arm; for love is as strong as death, Jealousy as cruel as the grave; its flames are flames of fire,*
A most vehement flame."» Song of Songs (8:6)

I remember that a few days before the Iraqi government fell we heard a rumor that any Iraqi family was caught aiding a foreigner or covering for him would be considered spies as well as associates of the American enemies and their house would be bombed with them in it. The day the Iraqi government fell I saw my foreign brother in Christ coming towards our house after he was released on April 9, 2003 but we were all released from prison a few days before him by US forces when they broke into the prisons. When I saw him, I ran and hugged him asking, "Where have you been? I thought they had deported you from the country" He said, "No, they transferred me to another prison and when I went to my residence I couldn't stay there because it was sealed by the intelligence and he had nowhere to stay. This is when I could say the test had begun. I had two choices; the first was to close my home door in the face of this brother to protect myself and my family from the bombing of the Iraqi government which still tried to resist the US forces that invaded the country, or to open the door of my home and place my life and the life of my family at risk. I quickly brought him in although the neighbors had seen me take him in and that was a risk itself because if they had said anything about it we would be risking death. When I brought in, my mother said, "Son, this is very dangerous because we might be bombed." My mother was thinking of a way out of this situation so I said to her, "Mom, this person has no place to stay and he should be treated as we would Christ in our house so if we die because we accept Christ in our home, it would be a source of pride for us because we would die for something that matters and more so I am sure that He who saved us from prison and from death will deliver us from this as well." Then, I took him to the second floor and hid him there for a few days so he wouldn't be seen by the neighbors or talked about until things settled down. Later, when everything was more stable and everyone knew that the Iraqi government wasn't able to protect itself any longer and that many had either fled the country or killed, only then were we able to exercise normal lives in the midst of war and ministry in front of everyone again.

My brothers and sisters in Christ, it was a difficult test but the Lord was with us and here we are today alive and well with the blessings of the Lord. The Lord that has been with us until now always will be because He is good and commanded us to love one another as He loved us. May we learn this lesson from the Lord who gave Himself for us that we may therefore love each other as He did, an honor that none of us deserves.

True believers of Christ and those who are saved by His blood and received forgiveness for their sins through faith in what He did for them are considered members in Christ's church on Earth (only them) who have been born from God and experienced salvation. They are as Christ on Earth whatever their nationality, culture, gender or color. *«"... but Christ is all and in all."» Colossians (3:11)* We should view each other in Christ and not in the flesh but in the spirit within us and learn to always love one another not only when circumstances are completely comfortable rather in need and tribulation and to help each other when we are able. *«"By this we know love, because He laid down His life for us. And we also ought to lay down our lives for the brethren. But whoever has this world's goods, and sees his brother in need, and shuts up his heart from him, how does the love of God abide in him? My little children, let us not love in word or in tongue, but indeed and in truth."» 1 John (3: 16-18)* rather we should love even when circumstances could lead us to losing our lives for each other as Christ did with us. *«"This is My commandment, that you love one another as I have loved you. Greater love has no one than this, <u>than to lay down one's life for his friends.</u>"» John (15: 12-13)* These are the new testament relationships built in the Holy Spirit among believers and which is founded on true love that emerges from God's spirit and which Christ practiced for us too. Let us follow His example.

"But none of these things move me; nor do I count my life dear to myself, so that I may finish my race with joy, and the ministry which I received from the Lord Jesus, to testify to the gospel of the grace of God", The book of Acts 20: 24

Some may think that I oppose a particular religion, denomination, faith or doctrine in writing this book. No dear reader. I am simply declaring the light I have been given and it is up to you (the reader) to ultimately and willfully decide and determine whether the light you have is true or a darkness that has deceived you for a long time even if you are a Christian.

One day, in prison, an intelligence officer asked one of the brothers with me a strange question, "Are you Muslim?" I admire the answer he gave him, "I am Muslim." although he was a Christian pastor. They asked, "Are you making fun of us?" He replied, "Do you know what being a Muslim means? 'Muslim' means one who has surrendered his life to God and lives for him. You kill, you are unjust, you commit adultery, smoke, get drunk and you do all that is distasteful, but I am just, I don't kill, nor commit adultery, or smoke and get drunk, or do any of your doings. Now, who is a true Muslim? You or me?" They replied, "To be honest, you are. Your Islam is real. Tell us how we can become real Muslims like you?" To that he replied, "You have to believe in Jesus Christ and you will be saved." And he began to explain to them the way to salvation through Jesus Christ. Some of them believed, some postponed the decision, and some rejected faith and left.

Dear reader, the issue isn't a race of religions, or which religion is the right one and which is wrong. Rather, it is a life lived in the way of God and with Him only through Jesus Christ and no other. He is the only one who can change a human being's life from the inside, creating a new heart and a new creature in Jesus Christ. *«"Therefore, if anyone is in Christ, he is a new creation; old things have passed away; behold, all things have become new."»* 2 Corinthians (5: 17)

When we were released and just before we left the Iraqi intelligence building, some officers asked us, "How do you behave this way? You were saying the same things. You protected each other and you never denied each other. You also never swear." The Iraqi intelligence officers were amazed at our behavior while in prison. To be honest, so were we after we had been released. We were truly one soul and one spirit in Him although we were apart from each other. *«"By this all will know that you are My disciples, if you have love for one another."»* John (13: 35) The Holy Spirit was guiding us and we didn't know it. This what Jesus said in *Matthew (10: 19-20)* *«"But when they deliver you up, do not worry about how or what you should speak. For it will be given to you in that hour what you should speak; for it is not you who speak, but the Spirit of your Father who speaks in you."».*

How I got saved (born again) experience

It is important that we chronicle the experiences that we go through with God in life so that they are not forgotten, because as human beings we tend to quickly forget what God has done and continues to do in our lives as the Israelites did when they were led out of Egypt, the land of oppression *«"They soon forgot His works..."» Psalm 106: 13*. Therefore, the word of God encourages us not to forget what He had done in our lives in the past and up until now, and to always remind ourselves of what He has done for us *«"Bless the Lord, O my soul, And forget not all His benefits"» Psalm 103: 2* This is what I personally attempt to do by documenting and recording what God has done in my life and to narrate it all to the coming generation in this book.

I was born in an Assyrian Orthodox Christian family, but I also spent 17 years in a Chaldean church after which I joined the Presbyterian Evangelical Church (where I got saved and believed in Jesus Christ as my Lord and savior) and Baptist Church. I also attended the Pentecostal Church, Charismatic Church, Prophetic and Apostolic Church, the Non-Denominational Church and Church of the Brethren among others. Even Jehovah's Witnesses attempted, on several occasions, to invite me to become a member of their misguiding, death-dealing teachings and meetings. However, as their cowardly nature doesn't serve them, they have never lasted for more than 5 minutes in a discussion with me nor do they know how or to where they should flee as a group, despite the fact that they would initiate the usually failing conversation with me.

Dear reader, as you move forward in reading my testimony, you will become aware that I was a tourist of different Christian denominations and churches for a number of years and in various countries such as Iraq, Jordan, Egypt, and the US. I do not favor any one Christian denomination over another here or prefer one to the other. Through my experience, I know very well that God does not favor any one religion, denomination or specific doctrine *«"In truth I perceive that God shows no partiality. But in every nation whoever fears Him and works righteousness is accepted by Him."» Acts 10: 34* Therefore, I believe that God has His people and followers everywhere as it is said in *Acts 18: 10 «"for I have many people in this city"»* …and that the kingdom of God will include all nations from every tribe, people, tongue and nation who believe in the blood of the Lord Jesus as the savior and redeemer of their lives *«"…and have redeemed us to God by Your blood Out of every tribe and tongue and people and nation…"» Revelation 5: 9*

During my childhood, I was always looking to satisfy the Lord in my life and I thought that it would be through fulfilling my duties and practicing all the rituals, customs and religious statutes of Christianity (as a Christian) like going to church (the Catholic church at the time), serving as an assistant deacon for the pastor, attending Christian festivals and religious events, including taking all the vows and adhering to many the fasting seasons, in addition to taking all the long walks for hours in order to perform what I thought would lead to the forgiveness of my many sins or reduce their punishment, and so on of rites that any devout could exercise in order to try to satisfy God by personal efforts, whether they be a Christian or a non-Christian. My repeated attempts to live according to what God wants from me, as usual, all failed, and I would grow increasingly more into evil and evil relationships with others. It would grow more and more inside me as I increased the sin in my life and in my relationships with evil people. I became more barbaric, brutal and cruel because of the sins and evil practices, which led to a hardening of my heart turning it to stone, without a sense of sin or guilt toward others. I was a live example of *«"If God puts no trust in His saints, and the heavens are not pure in His sight, how much less man, who is abominable and filthy, who drinks iniquity like water!"» Job 15: 15* Yes, I had been drinking iniquity like water until it reached an extreme degree of evil and disobedience and completely lost hope in life. I decided to commit suicide several times but I could not do it, so I said to myself, "Maybe if I die a martyr for Christianity, then I would enter paradise (and get eternal life) and be saved from hell and eternal punishment. Inside, I felt guilt, condemnation, shame and disgrace because of my uncountable sins. I was severely depressed and had lost all hope in life. From my point of view, I thought that martyrdom would be the only way to satisfy God and get Him to forgive my sins. I waited for the moment that I would die a martyr in the name of Christianity, as it was what I believed to be right at the time being a sinful human being distant from God and which I came to realize was all wrong later.

Dear reader, religiosity is an internal feeling not exclusive to Christianity, Islam, Buddhism or any other religion, sect or belief. It is a feeling inside every human being born on the face of this earth because it is as God says in ***Ecclesiastes 3: 11*** «*"...He has put eternity in their hearts..."*» Religiosity is man's attempt to reach God and please Him in a human way by the application of the commandments of men and not the commandments of God, «*"and in vain they worship Me, teaching as doctrines the commandments of men."*» ***Mark 7: 7*** this is demonstrated by hiding behind the guise of religion or other failing human practices, which is what happened in the beginning of creation with the first man, Adam. When Adam sinned, death poisoned him and as a result of this death, there came to be countless rational human attempts to save oneself from the judgment of God, all of which have failed. Adam tried all of these attempts from the beginning in the Garden of Eden and since we are the children of the first Adam, we have inherited this fallen nature and being dead and separated from God we try to do the same as he did. «***"Therefore, just as through one man sin entered the world, and death through sin, and thus death spread to all men, because all sinned"***» ***Romans 5: 12*** and «***"For if by the one man's offense death reigned through the one"***» ***Romans 5: 17*** We do not realize that

God has His own way to help us reach to Him, i.e. faith. «*"But without faith it is impossible to please Him"*» *Hebrews 11: 6*

When man makes a mistake, he immediately tries to justify his sin pushing it away from himself and blaming it on others and / or on oneself and increasing religious practices, acts of goodness and all that he assumes will contribute to his salvation. All that, just to get rid of the guilt and condemnation, which haunt him on the inside, even leading some to kill themselves and others in their belief that they serve God by doing so. *«"These things I have spoken to you; that you should not be made to stumble. They will put you out of the synagogues; yes, the time is coming that whoever kills you will think that he offers God service. And these things they will do to you because they have not known the Father nor Me. But these things I have told you, that when the time comes, you may remember that I told you of them."» John 16: 1-4* However, they are attempting to gain forgiveness in Adam's way, the useless religious and human way, finally reaching despair which misleads them into suicide believing they are now martyrs accepted by God, not knowing that the word "martyr" means "witness" which implies that the person "is killed for his testimony of truth", as in speaking the truth to many others who refuse it, provoking anger and increasing hatred towards that person leading to his murder because of his testimony of truth. This is what happened to all the true prophets and Jesus

Christ himself, who testified the truth in addition to Stephen, the first martyr in Christianity. *«"When they heard these things they were cut to the heart, and they gnashed at him with their teeth... Then they cried out with a loud voice, stopped their ears, and ran at him with one accord and they cast him out of the city and stoned him"» Acts 7: 54 & 57-58* True believers were killed because of their testimony of truth and never kill anyone at all. Therefore, dear reader, we now understand that the word "martyr" means "victim" (as in any person killed by others because of his spoken testimony of truth) not "culprit" (who kills others and claims martyrdom after his death for crimes he committed against others). A culprit is always the guilty one, a killer like his father the devil, as the bible states *«"You are of your father the devil, and the desires of your father you want to do. He was a murderer from the beginning..."» John 8: 44*

Going back now to fulfill my story, having lost hope in any way to obtain inner peace and get rid of the guilt of sin and its fatal weight, one day, almost midnight, I could not sleep because of a frequent power outage in Iraq (in Baghdad) and the mosquitoes were so disturbing that no one at home could sleep. I decided to sit outside with my brother where we listened to the battery radio. As my brother tuned for radio stations and we listened to different ones including songs, news and others, he passed one station incidentally passed one quickly as he heard a word from the bible and about Jesus Christ. I exclaimed "Wait! That station was talking about the bible and Jesus Christ. Go back." So he did, and we listened in on that station speaking the word of the bible and Christ. My brother said, "I have known about this station for a while." But he never used to listen to it. I replied, "Why didn't you ever tell me about it?" I learned the station's frequency and listened in every day at the same time for an hour and a half at midnight and again for half an hour early morning. I continued to listen to that station and encouraged my family to listen to it. A few months later, I experienced the following:

I was alone and sleeping on the sofa in the living room, when suddenly, and to my amazement, I saw myself outside my body at almost half a meter away and began to see everything around me including my body lying there on the sofa. I glanced at the living room clock and it was three in the morning and I realized with all my being that I was dead and here I was going to hell with no hope of coming back to life. That feeling and the truth that I had realized being with my full awareness, was so real that what we call reality is mere fantasy and illusion when compared to the truth and reality of that moment. Immediately, I began to cry and gnash my teeth fiercely, regretting that I hadn't repented of my sins feeling fully aware that I had left my body never to return to it again. Worst yet, I realized completely that I was about to spend the whole of eternity in hell. I bit my thumb in regret and sorrow which would do me no good. I truly experienced the sensation described in *Matthew 13: 40-42* «*"Therefore as the tares are gathered and burned in the fire, so it will be at the end of this age. The Son of Man will send out His angels, and they will gather out of His kingdom all things that offend, and those who practice lawlessness, and will cast them into the furnace of fire. There will be wailing and gnashing of teeth"*» It was indescribably horrific.

Dear reader, when I went through that, I had not received any teaching or preaching at church that instructed me that if I didn't repent I would go to hell or any other eternal matters that every human being will experience after departing their current body through death. I only felt it as a regular sinful human inside me. Experiencing that bitter real moment, I truly realized that there is a place called hell and this is a message to anyone who doesn't believe in the reality of eternal fire to repent and turn away from their wrongful thinking in this regard as the bible clearly spoke about it and Jesus Christ personally taught about it. Please note that many misleading Christian denominations today do not believe in the reality and existence of hell where they will spend their eternity for not believing what the Lord is says in His word, the Bible. The Lord allowed me to experience this test to be a salvation for the pure of heart and an announcement death to the wicked, not that they may repent, but for my words to bear witness against them on judgment day, which is inevitably close. They will receive their punishment here on earth before they go to their eternal doom for everyone to see. After having this out body experience and fully realizing the damnation I was headed, I suddenly found myself back in my body and leaped up absolutely terrified with a profound knowledge throughout my entire being that the Lord had permitted my return to my body and gave me life. I rose up from the sofa immediately and liked around. I found everything exactly as I had seen it when I left my body and it really was 3 in the morning. So, I knew that what I had experienced was real, and that the Lord, out of His love for me, had given me a second chance in life.

I looked at my pillow, which was soaked in tears, and felt the pain in my thumb, which I had so bitterly bitten. That, too, was real. I fell to my knees and thanked the Lord for giving me a second chance in life in order to come back and be with Him. Although, as you will come to see, I didn't know should be done to be saved from that eternal hell. I continued to listen to that Christian radio station regularly, but I hadn't yet experienced what the bible calls "born again" or "salvation". One day, I ran into one of my dearest friends at the institute I attended at the time and asked, "Do you know that Christian radio station that speaks of the bible and Christ?" He replied, "Of course I know it." So, I asked him, "Why didn't you ever tell me about it?" The same question I had asked my brother when he said he knew about a while back.

(Dear reader, I would like to add a simple note; the very little that you know could benefit someone else, so don't be stingy with what you know to anyone, and don't undermine what the Lord reveals to you, because it is not for you alone but others as well. That is one purpose for this book.)

After inquiring from my friend if had known about this station, I asked him, "Then, why don't the churches we attend regularly teach any of these teachings about the gospel and Christ?" Back then, I was part of a liturgical church that only taught rituals and Christian statutes. I had been going to that church for nearly 17 years without knowing Christ personally because there wasn't any preaching of Christ, only the dead like religious practice of Christian rituals that do not benefit anyone as they truly are not from the Lord as it is said in *Jeremiah 23: 32* «*"Yet I did not send them or command them; therefore they shall not profit this people at all."*»

I even asked an elderly woman one day after I had experienced salvation, "Were you born from above or not?" She replied, "I am a Christian and I have served my whole life in the church, but what is being born again?" She had never heard the message of salvation or the true gospel even though she had been a servant of the church her whole life. My question here is; what kind of church doesn't preach the word of God and that salvation is through Christ alone? What kind of church is basically darkness with only rituals, statutes and religious appearances, when it should be the light for people? The bible says, «*"Do not be carried about with various and strange doctrines. For, it is good that the heart be established by grace, not with foods which have not profited those who have been occupied with them."*» *Hebrews 13:9*

I was one day a victim of those buildings and structures that claim to be Christian, but I never came to know Christ in them. I did not enjoy the freedom of salvation because the Holy Spirit did not reside in those Christian buildings and ministries, who in my opinion "claim" to be Christian churches, because if they were truly full of the Spirit, myself and others would have enjoyed real freedom as a result to experiencing the Lord's salvation. The bible puts it this way, *«"Now the Lord is the Spirit; and where the Spirit of the Lord is, there is liberty."» 2 Corinthians 3:17* and I was still bound by sin, *«"Jesus answered them, "Most assuredly, I say to you, whoever commits sin is a slave of sin"» John 8: 34.* This does not mean that if you were born again you will never make mistakes; it means that you are not a slave of that sin unless you allow it to control you. Therefore the bible says, *«"Therefore do not let sin reign in your mortal body, that you should obey it in its lusts. And do not present your members as instruments of unrighteousness to sin, but present yourselves to God as being alive from the dead, and your members as instruments of righteousness to God. For sin shall not have dominion over you, for you are not under law but under grace."» Romans 6: 12-14* and *«"nor give place to the devil"» Ephesians 4: 27* If we willfully give place to the devil, he will happily take advantage of that opportunity and do as he pleases with our lives. That is what I have come to experience personally in many situations. For that reason, we should not give him a chance to do so, that is by remaining pure and staying away from his only method of destruction for us; disbelief of the word of God. The result will always be sin. *«"For whatever is not from faith is sin."» Romans 14: 23*. The churches that were supposed to be light for people have become in the most part full of darkness and corruption. Jesus said, *«"You are the salt of the earth; but if the salt loses its flavor, how shall it be seasoned? It is then good for nothing but to be thrown out and trampled underfoot by men."» Matthew 5: 13* Most churches nowadays have been corrupted by their own teachings which they receive from within themselves or society, traditions, customs, philosophies or doctrines, and not from the word of God. The bible describes them as, *«"and in vain they worship Me, teaching as doctrines the commandments of men."» Mark 7: 7* and *«"and my speech and my preaching were not with persuasive words of human wisdom, but in demonstration of the Spirit and of power, that your faith should not be in the wisdom of men but in the power of God."» 1 Corinthians 2:4-5*. The words of human philosophers have nothing to do with the demonstration of the Spirit and Its power, rather it works against The Spirit. No wonder then, that many people hate even the true Church and reject the Christian faith because they were first exposed to a false church that has been tainted and trampled on by people. It is only natural to reject such Christian faith because false teachers and fake messengers from Satan, inside the church, are employed to be a stumbling block for many, as Jesus predicted *«"Then He said to the disciples, "It is impossible that no offenses should come, but woe to him through whom they do come! It would be better for him if a millstone were hung around his neck, and he were thrown into the sea, than that he should offend one of these little ones. Take heed to yourselves. If your brother sins against you, rebuke him; and if he repents, forgive him."» Luke 17: 1-3* If one is able to escape the liturgical churches that do not preach the true gospel by experiencing salvation and being born again, you will find that he would face other difficulties in several other churches, where there are people who are resist the Holy Spirit and Its work that is evident through signs and miracles of the power of God's word. As for my personal experience, I have found that humans always want to limit God in a certain doctrine, and turn a particular experience done by God in their lives into a final stage of their spiritual lives, unaware that God only begins with the first step in the life of a Christian believer, namely salvation and second birth, then bringing him/her gradually to the very purpose of faith and salvation through his/her journey in life, as he did with the children of Israel in the wilderness. Their exodus from Egypt was not the final step in their lives, but it was God's purpose for them to enter into the Promised Land. Although, in reality, many will fail as the bible declares, *«"But with most of them God was not well pleased, for their bodies were scattered in the wilderness."»* *1 Corinthians 10: 5* (The wilderness being their journey in Christian faith) Only a few will be victorious and obtain glory and honor from the Lord Jesus personally as described in *Revelation 2&3* *«"... To him who overcomes..."»* The Lord's reward is for all those who have endured until the end and found victorious, only because many will be defeated. I encourage you, dear reader, to remain fixed in Christ and his word until the very end because your reward will be from Christ personally. The devil has deceived and continues to deceive many. The churches which call for redemption only are deceived by resisting the churches that call for the baptism of water, and churches that baptize with water are deceived by resisting churches that believe in the baptism of the Holy Spirit, speaking in tongues and the gifts of the Holy Spirit, including other various means of deception. Not to mention churches who teach only rituals, as I do not see the difference between them and any other pagan temple, or between their leaders and those who indeed worship idols. Unfortunately, they claim that they are Christians; rather they are false Christians and pitfalls for many. It is an opportunity today and now for everyone to turn back from these denominations and Christian doctrines to the Word of God, the Bible, and to preaching Jesus Christ as Lord, savior, redeemer and mediator for all of us human beings before God. I encourage everyone to take the chance today and turn back to that corner stone, which is the rock of our salvation for all of us. I give thanks to God that He still gives us time to return and repent from dead works, as the Lord Himself says that he has overlooked times of ignorance «*"... because He has appointed a day on which He will judge the world in righteousness by the Man whom He has ordained. He has given assurance of this to all by raising Him from the dead."*» *Acts 17: 30-31.* Returning to my testimony, my friend had promised to take me to the church that preaches the bible and Christ, but he never did for months. During that time I was committed to listening to that radio station, but I hadn't yet experienced salvation and true change of heart. One day, I was at a very low point and had been fighting with everyone at home, when my friend came over to take me to church. I said, "I don't want to go with you to church, especially today because I have quarreled with my whole family and cause d much hurt for them. Today I am not ready to go to church at all." I was relying completely on my state, dear reader, and my works, whether good or bad, in choosing to go to church, and I told my friend to leave and go without me, but he persisted in persuading me to go with him, and having come a long way to take me, I decided to go with him out of courtesy for him and his sister, who came with him. That was the first time in my life to hear the word of God and Christ being preached in church.

I was very happy with the hymns and the preacher was speaking to hundreds of young people my age. I was around 21 years old then. His words were directed to everyone, "Do you want to begin the New Year with Jesus or do you want to go on as you are and this next year will be like all the other years that have passed in your life?" The preacher was asking that question because we were about to enter the New Year in 2000 and that meeting was two days before New Year's Eve. Suddenly, there was a scream inside of me that I do not want my life to continue as it was in the past. I recalled my life in a moment and felt that I do not want to continue in that hell any longer; rather I want Jesus to enter my life and change it that minute!

After making that decision in my heart, the meeting ended and as my friend and I left, I felt that something different had occurred inside me. I felt that I wanted to fly up in the air out of joy and peace which came over me and filled my heart. It was such a profound feeling as I had not known the meaning of such feelings before. I looked directly at my friend and asked him, "Do you feel what I feel?" He replied in wonder, "No, what do you feel?" I answered, "I am so happy, I can soar up in the air." My friend was used to the meetings and didn't take much importance to what I said. I know exactly what I felt back then, but I didn't understand what really happened with me. I entered the church depressed, sad, full of guilt and heavy with the burden of sin inside with the stingy feeling of condemnation, loss, death and hell. As I left, I was full of peace, joy, happiness and fatherly forgiveness. I decided to attend the meeting in that church every week since then, and later realized that I had experienced being born again which is a gracious gift from God to whoever receives Christ as savior in his/her life.

Dear reader, all religions and human doctrines, including Christianity, are not able to create such a miracle in a human being's life. Therefore, salvation comes only through faith in Jesus Christ as a personal savior as he tasted death on behalf of every human *«"…. by the grace of God, might taste death for everyone."» Hebrews 2: 9* so that whoever believes in Him will not perish, but receives everlasting life, *«"For God so loved the world that He gave His only begotten Son, that whoever believes in Him should not perish but have everlasting life" John 3: 16.* I began my journey with the Lord ever since, reading His word and attending the meetings at that church back then. I was very passionate about sharing what God had done in my life that it affected everyone around me at home, my friends and even my enemies. All I knew was **(I love Jesus whom loved me and gave His life for me)** and that *«… though I was blind, now I see!"» John 9:25* in addition to *«"He has delivered us from the power of darkness and conveyed us into the kingdom of the Son of His love"» Colossians 1: 13* therefore, *«"because the love of God has been poured out in our hearts by the Holy Spirit who was given to us. For when we were still without strength, in due time Christ died for the ungodly."» Romans 5: 5-6* I didn't think about anything except Jesus and His love for me. That was truly my honeymoon in my new relationship with the Lord who loved me, but it did not last for long when I started relating with religious Christians around me. I was like a child who accepts any teaching and any minister who speaks of the Lord, without distinguishing what was truly the word of God and what was human teaching and demonic teaching. Thanks to the Lord who remained faithful to me until now and will remain that way forever because of His faithfulness and eternal love for me. Dear reader, I didn't know exactly what my experience was called, but I later learned that it is called salvation. I tried to understand it with my mind, but I found it difficult to grasp in the human mind because as Christ said, *«"The wind blows where it wishes, and you hear the sound of it, but cannot tell where it comes from and where it goes. So is everyone who is born of the Spirit."» John 3: 8* even one of my Muslim friends asked me, "Fadi, what is going on with you?" Unlike before, I was resisting sin in my life and lost all desire for it. I no longer accepted it or enjoyed it as I used to, so, I answered him, "I really don't know what has happened to me. All I know is that I love Jesus." So he asked, "What are you reading?" I said, "The bible" and he said, "Can you give me one to read, and I will give it back to you later?" So, I gave him a bible and three days later he came to me and said, "I read the whole bible, from the beginning to the end, and nothing happened to me like you.

All I read about were stories of this guy and that guy." I immediately knew that he did not understand what had happened with me, and I couldn't describe it in a rational and human way in order for him to understand. That experience only comes through faith in Jesus and what He did for us in on the cross and our acceptance of that truth in faith as children do, not our studies or works or limited human mind. Therefore, the topic of salvation and being reborn was a difficult one for Nicodemus, who tried to limit the word of God with his own limited human mind, but couldn't. One day, I attended a meeting that unfortunately claims to be a Christian one and which teaches salvation through philosophy and rationalism. They teach that there are a number of steps you have to go through in order to obtain salvation, and I went through a phase of doubt, fear and mental paralysis doubting even my own salvation. I realized that this salvation they are preaching is very difficult when taught the way they do; as some say that first you have to repent then believe, while others say that you have to believe then repent, all of course, is based on verses from the bible. But God made the matter a miracle that only occurs in a man's life through the acceptance of God's free grace in faith as a child. *«"and said, (that is Jesus said) "Assuredly, I say to you, unless you are converted and become as little children, you will by no means enter the kingdom of heaven."» Matthew 18:3.*

Repentance doesn't mean that one leaves his sins; rather it means that he changes his way of thinking from one thing to another and changes his view of God from a just judge into a kind loving father. This only takes place through the word of God and His Spirit, not through the word of God and the human mind. I remember that when I came to believe in Jesus, all I experienced was happiness, joy and forgiveness, and that all of my burdens of sin had been lifted as Jesus said, *«"Come to Me, all you who labor and are heavy laden, and I will give you rest."» Matthew 11: 28* I really did experience comfort as He said and for a long time, I would wake in the middle of the night to sing to the Lord and bitterly cry as if I was being cleansed on the inside and purified as the bible says, *«".. But you were washed, but you were sanctified, but you were justified in the name of the Lord Jesus and by the Spirit of our God."» 1 Corinthians 6: 11* I had truly become whiter than snow, just as the bible describes in *Psalm 51: 7, «"... Wash me, and I shall be whiter than snow."»* and *«"'Come now, and let us reason together', says the Lord, 'Though your sins are like scarlet, they shall be as white as snow; though they are red like crimson, they shall be as wool'."» Isaiah 1: 18* I never once thought of turning away from my sins, until I came to Jesus. The sins that I had committed for 21 years were completely erased from my memory and no longer had an effect on my life, and when asked about them I would reply, "That person is dead, and you are speaking to a new person" I also calculate my age starting at 21, that is the age I received salvation, not my birth years. *«"For I will forgive their iniquity, and their sin I will remember no more"» Jeremiah 31: 34, «"Repent therefore and be converted, that your sins may be blotted out"» Acts 3:19* True repentance is knowing Jesus and what he has done for us on the cross, which in turn leads to returning to God knowing that He loves us. Until this day, I don't recall being condemned or guilty of any sin I have ever committed up until 21 because Jesus has cleansed me completely. *«"And the blood of Jesus Christ His Son cleanses us from all sin"» 1 John 1: 7* and also, *«"and from Jesus Christ, the faithful witness, the firstborn from the dead, and the ruler over the kings of the earth. To Him who loved us and <u>washed us from our sins in His own blood</u>"» Revelation 1: 5* I became entirely focused on Jesus and His love for me, and I fell so in love with God for flooding me with forgiveness for my many sins. *«"Therefore I say to you, <u>her sins, which are many, are forgiven, for she loved much.</u> But to whom little is forgiven, the same loves little."» Luke 7:47* I really did feel as if I was the worst sinner in my generation just as Paul felt in his time describing what he felt in *1 Timothy 1: 15-16* *«"This is a faithful saying and worthy of all acceptance, that Christ Jesus came into the world to save sinners, of whom I am chief. However, for this reason I obtained mercy, that in me first Jesus Christ might show all longsuffering, as a pattern to those who are going to believe on Him for everlasting life."»* God truly poured a miraculous love in my heart for Him, *«"Now hope does not disappoint, because the love of God has been poured out in our hearts by the Holy Spirit who was given to us."»* *Romans 5:5* I no longer viewed God as a judge that I should fear; rather a <u>kind loving father</u> who *«"As far as the east is from the west, So far has He removed our transgressions from us. As a father pities his children, So the Lord pities those who fear Him"»* *Psalm 103:12-13* I believe this exactly what the bible meant in *John 1: 12* *«"But as many as received Him (as in believed in Jesus), to them He gave the right to become children of God"»* that means we will be able to see God as a loving father after we accept Jesus *«"All things have been delivered to Me by My Father, and no one knows the Son except the Father. Nor does anyone know the Father except the Son, and the one to whom the Son wills to reveal Him."»* *Matthew 11: 27* My faith in Jesus revealed the truth about

God the father for I never would have known Him unless I met Jesus because Jesus is the only way to knowing God as a loving father. *«"Jesus said to him, "I am the way, the truth, and the life. No one comes to the Father except through Me"» John 14: 6* Only then did my personality completely change because my view of God's personality, and whoever came into contact with me during that time would wonder what had happened to me, as I did not just practice sin, I was a teacher of sin for those around me before I was saved. For that reason, the affect that being saved had on my life was immensely strong, especially during the first three years of my new life and until I joined the school of religious and false teachers of the church whom you have read about here. My spiritual life deteriorated and the Lord recovered me again to serve Him and witness about it. May all glory be His forever and ever. Amen. *«"and when you have returned to Me, strengthen your brethren"» Luke 22: 32* That is why I attempt to chronicle through these few pages; testify about the grace of God in my life.

Salvation and being born again is a real experience that any human being can willfully try. Our first birth into this world was not by our will, but by the will of our father and mother. We did not have any choice in our fathers or mothers, or where and how we were born. However, in this second birth, it is with our personal choice, where we can accept it or deny it and it all depends on the person's preference. The only way for a second birth is through faith in Jesus Christ. *«"He was in the world, and the world was made through Him, and the world did not know Him. He came to His own, and His own did not receive Him. But as many as received Him, to them He gave the right to become children of God, to those who believe in His name: who were born, not of blood, nor of the will of the flesh, nor of the will of man, but of God."» John (1: 10-13)*

One day, I was sitting in a church that Pastor Gregory led speaking about how he experienced faith more than 30 years ago in the United States as the Holy Spirit revealed to me the dimensions of the story of my salvation, which was quite similar to the testimony of Pastor Gregory, and which I had experienced only 15 years ago. I said to myself: "It is imperative that this be real and with no doubt for everyone who believes. How can this person spiritually experience something more than 30 years ago quite similar to what I experienced only 15 years ago, and with him living in the United States and I live in Iraq? The Holy spirit really does work in different times and various countries and places with whoever believes in Jesus." This testimony has been experienced by millions and millions of people across generations and is still available for anyone who believes in Jesus as Savior and Lord of his life.

God bless your life.

Live evidence of the appearance of Jesus in modern day times

... As for the appearance of Jesus to my cell mate in prison, it is considered a distinguishing line of the true living Jesus Christ from any religion, denomination, sect or faith even if they claim to be Christian. Jesus is alive forever as it is written of Him in *Hebrews 13: 8* «*"Jesus Christ is the same yesterday, today, and forever."*» This is a characteristic that God alone enjoys; there is no difference between God the Father and God the Son, Jesus, when it comes to divinity as they are both one, just as there is no difference between water and ice in substance. Jesus Himself said «*"I and My Father are one."*» *John 10:30* He proves that He is alive today by appearing to many around the world, now and until His coming, proving His resurrection from the dead when He appeared to the two women on their way to Galilee to tell the disciples that Jesus had risen from the dead just as the angel had told them and as it is written *Matthew 28: 9-10* «*"Jesus met them, saying, "Rejoice!" So they came and held Him by the feet and worshiped Him. Then Jesus said to them, "Do not be afraid. Go and tell My brethren to go to Galilee, and there they will see Me."*» Then He appeared to Mary Magdalene «*"Now when He rose early on the first day of the week, He appeared first to Mary Magdalene,"*»

Mark 16: 9 «*"she turned around and saw Jesus standing there, and did not know that it was Jesus."*» *John 20:14* He also appeared to two disciples looking differently «*"After that, He appeared in another form to two of them as they walked and went into the country."*» *Mark 16:12* ... «*"While they were talking and discussing these things, Jesus himself approached them and walked with them, But their eyes were denied identify him"*» *Luke 24: 15-16* And since Jesus appears, He also disappears «*"Then their eyes were opened and they knew Him; and He vanished from their sight."*» *Luke 24: 31* He also appeared to seven of His disciples all together «*"... Jesus showed Himself again to the disciples at the Sea of Tiberias,"*» *John 21: 1* As «*"This is now the third time Jesus showed Himself to His disciples after He was raised from the dead."*» *John 21:14*. He also appeared to the 11 disciples «*".. Jesus came and stood in the midst, and said to them, "Peace be with you." »* *John 20:19* ... «*"An finally, He appeared to the eleven as they sat at the table;"*» *Mark 16:14* ... «*"Jesus Himself stood in the midst of them, ,and said to them, "Peace to you."*» *Luke 24: 36*, «*"... Jesus came, the doors being shut, and stood in the midst, and said, "Peace to you!"*» *John 20:26*

The message of Jesus' appearances is still resisted to this day by everyone and even by many Christian believers, leaders and ministers as well as non-Christians. This is not new or strange, as it was suffered by those closest to Him and even His disciples and true messengers. Take a look at their reactions when they heard that He was alive and that He had appeared to others:

- They had doubts ... «*"When they saw Him, <u>but some doubted."</u>» Matthew 28: 17*

- «*"And when they heard that He was alive and had been seen by her, they did not believe"» Mark 16:11*

- They also did not believe ... «*"And they went and told it to the rest, but they <u>did not believe them either"</u>» Mark 16:13*

- They did not believe and were amazed ... «*"... He showed them His hands and His feet. But while they still did not believe for joy, <u>and marveled"</u>» Luke 24: 40*

- They did not believe ... «*"And their words seemed to them like idle tales, <u>and they did not believe them."</u>» Luke 24: 11*

- They were afraid and they thought they saw a ghost ... «*"But they were terrified and frightened, <u>and supposed they had seen a spirit."</u>» Luke 24: 37*

- The apostle Thomas did not believe in the appearance of Jesus unless he personally saw and touched Him with his hands ... *"The other disciples therefore said to him (That is Thomas), "We have seen the Lord."* » But he said to them: "Unless I see in His hands the print of the nails, and put my finger into the print of the nails, and put my hand into His side, I will not believe." John 20:25

And now take a look at how Jesus responded to their lack of faith and belief that He is alive and that He had appeared to others as a sign of His resurrection from the dead:

- Jesus and His reprimand to those who did not believe His appearance after His resurrection ... «*"Later He appeared to the eleven as they sat at the table; and <u>He rebuked their unbelief and hardness of heart</u>, because they <u>did not believe</u> those who had seen Him after He had risen."*» *Mark 16: 14*

- Jesus reprimanded the stupidity (of those who were supposed to be believers) for their disbelief that He had appeared to others ... «*"Then He said to them, <u>"O foolish ones, and slow of heart to believe</u> in all that the prophets have spoken!"*» *Luke 24: 25*

- Jesus rebuked them for skepticism even as He appeared to them personally ... «*"And He said to them, <u>"Why are you troubled? And why do doubts arise in your hearts?"</u>*» *Luke 24: 38*

- Jesus reprimanded the Apostle Thomas ... «*"Then He said to Thomas, "Reach your finger here, and look at My hands; and reach your hand here, and put it into My side. Do not be unbelieving, but believing." And Thomas answered and said to Him, "My Lord and my God!" Jesus said to him, "Thomas, because you have seen Me, you have believed. Blessed are those who have not seen and yet have believed."» John 20: 27-29*

We believe in Jesus, even though we have not seen Him with our own eyes. Rather if we see Him with our own eyes, this will give us an additional living testimony and evidence of Him being alive and that He rose from the dead.

As usual, those who do not have a good knowledge and a full view of the word of God (the Bible) might say that Jesus had ascended to heaven, and after His ascension and seating at the right hand of God, He no longer appears to people here on Earth, and that He will return one more time to Earth for His second coming only, citing the word of God as follows: *«"**Then** if anyone says to you, 'Look, here is the Christ!' or 'There!' do not believe it. For false christs and false prophets will rise and show great signs and wonders to deceive, if possible, even the elect. See, I have told you beforehand. "Therefore if they say to you, 'Look, He is in the desert!' do not go out; or 'Look, He is in the inner rooms!' do not believe it. For as the lightning comes from the east and flashes to the west, so also will the coming of the Son of Man be. For wherever the carcass is, there the eagles will be gathered together. "Immediately after the tribulation of those days the sun will be darkened, and the moon will not give its light; the stars will fall from heaven, and the powers of the heavens will be shaken. Then the sign of the Son of Man will appear in heaven, and then all the tribes of the earth will mourn, and they will see the Son of Man coming on the clouds of heaven with power and great glory. And He will send His angels with a great sound of a trumpet, and they will gather together His elect from the four winds, from* *one end of heaven to the other"» Matthew 24: 23-31*

Note, dear reader, in this part, the first word Jesus begins with is the word "***Then***" that means, there will be many events that occur between verse 5 and 22 in ***Matthew 24*** before the deceived begin to say «"'***Look, here is the Christ!' or 'There!'***'"» <u>Only then,</u> we should not believe what those deceivers say. These events have not occurred yet but they are very close, and the second coming of Jesus to Earth will be seen by everyone, not in some scattered geographical locations, but everyone on the face of the planet will see Him publicly coming on heavenly clouds, believers or non-believers, even His opponents. However, for now, I speak of His daily appearances in the lives of many as proof that He is alive, and not about His final coming to this world, which will be rather soon.

Read the following from the Word of God - The Bible - on the apparitions of Jesus and His angels, even after His ascension into heaven and seating at the right hand of God the Father and the sending of the Holy Spirit at Pentecost.

Jesus appeared to the greatest apostle of Christianity, Paul, as follows:

1. Jesus appeared to Saul (the greatest apostle and witness for Christ who wrote most of the letters in the Bible's New Testament)

«"As he journeyed he came near Damascus, and suddenly <u>*a light shone around him from heaven.*</u> *Then he fell to the ground, and heard a voice saying to him, "Saul, Saul, why are you persecuting Me?" And he said, "Who are You, Lord?" Then the Lord said,* <u>*"I am Jesus, whom you*</u> <u>*are persecuting.*</u> *"Arise and go into the city, and you will be told what you must do."» Acts 9: 3-6*

2. Jesus appeared in a vision to Ananias, one of the pupils and gave him guidance on what should be done *«"Now there* *was a certain disciple at Damascus named Ananias;* <u>*and*</u> <u>*to him the Lord said in a vision,*</u> *"Ananias." And he said, "Here I am, Lord. "So the Lord said to him, "Arise and go to the street called Straight, and inquire at the house of Judas for one called Saul of Tarsus, for behold, he is praying. And in a vision he has seen a man named Ananias coming in and putting his hand on him, so that he might receive his sight." Then Ananias answered, "Lord, I have heard from many about this man, how much harm he has done to Your saints in Jerusalem. And here he has authority from the chief priests to bind all who call on Your name." But the Lord said to him, "Go, for he is a chosen vessel of Mine to bear My name before Gentiles, kings, and the children of Israel. For I will show him how many things he must suffer for My name's sake." And Ananias went his way and entered the house;*

and laying his hands on him he said, "Brother Saul, the Lord Jesus, who appeared to you on the road as you came, has sent me that you may receive your sight and be filled with the Holy Spirit."» Acts 9: 10-17

3. The testimony of others that Saul had already seen the Lord ... *«"But Barnabas took him* (i.e. he took Saul, who is called the apostle Paul later) *and brought him to the apostles. And he declared to them how he had seen the Lord on the road, and that He had spoken to him,"» Acts 9:27*

4. The appearance of angels from God, even after Jesus ascended to heaven and the descent of the Holy Spirit *«"... About the ninth hour of the day he saw clearly in a vision an angel of God coming in and saying to him, "Cornelius!" And when he observed him, he was afraid, and said, "What is it, lord?" So he said to him, "Your prayers and your alms have come up for a memorial before God. Now send men to Joppa, and send for Simon whose surname is Peter.. He is lodging with Simon, a tanner, whose house is by the sea."» Acts 10: 3-6*

5. The Apostle Paul's testimony and his belief in the appearance of Jesus to the apostles, disciples and brothers in addition to his assertion of Jesus' appearance to him as well *«"He was seen by Cephas, then by the twelve. After that He was seen by over five hundred brethren at once,*

of whom the greater part remain to the present, After that He was seen by James, then by all the apostles. Then last of all He was seen by me also, as by one born out of due time!"» 1 Corinthians 15: 5-8.

Some Christian leaders are skeptics as well as those who are led by corrupt minds, their rational philosophy which stems from their Psyche and not the spirit of God as they teach their followers that Jesus only appeared in the days of the apostles and that we no longer need His appearance today. I would simply confront them and say, yes, you are right, you really don't need Jesus to appear to you, and He never will, to you or any of your followers because *«"But woe to you, scribes and Pharisees, hypocrites! For you shut up the kingdom of heaven against men; for you neither go in yourselves, nor do you allow those who are entering to go in."» Matthew 23:13* Therefore, you will not see the King in the kingdom of God, namely Lord Jesus, because you do not love Him, although you speak of Him and preach of Him to your followers in your churches, platforms and religious synagogues because you *«"... unless you are converted and become as little children, you will by no means enter the kingdom of heaven."» Matthew 18: 3.* Also, if He shows Himself to you, it will be in reproach as he did with my cell mate, or with His disciples and apostles for their disbelief that He was alive after His resurrection from the dead, and used His appearances as proof of that. Although Jesus is not obliged to appear to you, just as He didn't reveal Himself after His resurrection to the leaders of the Jews and religious people who crucified Him. Rather, He appeared only to His loved ones, whom He promised to return again after His resurrection and whom He invited to serve Him.

Jesus loves to appear to those who love Him, who love His appearing to them « *"... And he who loves Me will be loved by My Father, and I will love him and manifest Myself to him."* **John 14:21**. Here, Jesus was talking about His appearance to those who He loves and proof of this is when one of His disciples immediately asked Him in the following verse « *"Lord, <u>how is it that You will manifest Yourself to us,</u> and not to the world?"* **John 14:22** so, « *"Jesus answered and said to him, "If anyone loves Me, he will keep My word; and My Father will love him, and We will come to him and make Our home with him."* **John 14:23** Here, Jesus speaks about His appearance and His coming with God the father personally to whom He loves not about the Holy Spirit, whose coming He promised would follow His ascension to heaven. Whoever would love to see Jesus appear today, would also long to see Him come as a sovereign judging Lord, for there are people who are indeed happy to have seen Jesus appear to them and I am one of them. It is written of such people « *"... but also to all who have loved His appearing"* **2 Timothy 4: 8**

Jesus has told us believers that He would be present in every meeting we have in His name, and that promise became valid the day we believed in Him and to the end of the world « *"For where two or three are gathered together in My name, I am there in the midst of them."*» *Matthew 18:20* « *"... teaching them to observe all things that I have commanded you; and lo, I am with you always, even to the end of the age."*» *Matthew 28: 20.* However, in *John 14: 18-19* He speaks of His personal appearances after His death and resurrection where He cannot be seen by others, but by believers only « *"I will not leave you orphans; I will come to you. "A little while longer and the world will see Me no more, but you will see Me. Because I live, you will live also."*» Jesus spoke to His disciples a lot about His death and resurrection long before they occurred, but they did not understand what he was saying. Frankly, at first, I also did not understand how Jesus' apparitions to people could be evidence that He is risen from the dead and alive today. When my Muslim Sheikh cell mate told me that he had seen Jesus and that Jesus spoke to him, I too said "You are blessed because you saw Jesus and you are a Muslim, while I am a Christian, and still have never seen Him." However, I believe, dear reader, that Jesus will show Himself to me also here on Earth, because he declared that it is His desire to do so for those who love Him and love

His appearing to them.

Here are some verses from the Bible - the word of God-which witness that Jesus (the Son of man) had predicted His death and resurrection long before it happened:

«*"Now while they were staying in Galilee, Jesus said to them, "The Son of Man is about to be betrayed into the hands of men, and they will kill Him, and the third day He will be raised up." And they were exceedingly sorrowful."*» *Matthew 17: 22-23*

«*".. I and all things that are written by the prophets concerning the Son of Man will be accomplished. For He will be delivered to the Gentiles and will be mocked and insulted and spit upon. <u>He will be delivered to the Gentiles and will be mocked and insulted and spit upon. And the third day He will rise again.</u> But they understood none of these things; this saying was hidden from them, and they did not know the things which were spoken."*» *Luke 18: 31-34*

«*"For as Jonah was three days and three nights in the belly of the great fish, <u>so will the Son of Man be three days and three nights in the heart of the earth.</u>"*» *Matthew 12:40*

«"Behold, we are going up to Jerusalem, and the Son of Man will be betrayed to the chief priests and to the scribes; and they will condemn Him to death and deliver Him to the Gentiles; and they will mock Him, and scourge Him, and spit on Him, <u>and kill Him. And the third day He will rise again.</u>"» Mark 10: 33-34

«"And He began to teach them that the Son of Man must suffer many things, and be rejected by the elders and chief priests and scribes, and be killed, and after three days rise again."» Mark 8:31

«"From that time Jesus began to show to His disciples that He must go to Jerusalem, and suffer many things from the elders and chief priests and scribes, <u>and be killed, and be raised the third day.</u>"» Matthew 16:21

«".. For He <u>taught</u> His disciples and said to them, "The Son of Man is being betrayed into the hands of men, <u>and they will kill Him. And after He is killed, He will rise the third day."</u> But they did not understand this saying, and were afraid to ask Him."» Mark 9: 31-32.

Jesus said to the Jews who wanted to kill Him in *John 7:19* *«"... Why do you seek to kill Me? "... "I know that you are Abraham's descendants, <u>but you seek to kill Me,</u> because My word has no place in you."... "<u>But now you seek to kill Me,"</u>» John 8:37, 40* He explained why they want to kill him, saying: «*"You are of your father the devil, and the desires of your father you want to do. <u>He was a murderer from the beginning,"</u>» John 8:44*

Even outsiders knew that the Jews wanted to kill Jesus «*"Now some of them from Jerusalem said, <u>"Is this not He whom they seek to kill?"</u>» John 7:25*

The prophecy of Caiaphas, the high priest, of the death of Jesus: «*"... nor do you consider that it is expedient for us <u>that one man should die for the people,</u> and not that the whole nation should perish. Now this he did not say on his own authority; but being high priest that year he prophesied that Jesus would die for the nation, and not for that nation only, but also that He would gather together in one the children of God who were scattered abroad. Then, from that day on, <u>they plotted to put Him to death.""</u>» John 11: 50-53*

Jesus predicted the day they shroud Him: «*"But Jesus said, "Let her alone; she<u> has kept this</u> for the day of My burial."» John 12: 7*

«"Most assuredly, I say to you, unless a grain of wheat falls into the ground and dies, it remains alone; but if it dies, it produces much grain."» John 12:24

Jesus came for this hour, to die for every human being on the face of the Earth, and He voluntarily chose to do that *«"Now My soul is troubled, and what shall I say? 'Father, save Me from this hour'? But for this purpose I came to this hour."» John 12:27*

He also spoke of His death and burial in the tomb *«"... this for the day of My burial""» John 12: 7*

«"And I, if I am lifted up from the earth, will draw all peoples to Myself.. This He said, signifying by what death He would die."» John 12: 32-33

«"... Jesus knew that His hour had come that He should depart from this world to the Father,"» John 13: 1

Jesus declared that He would die and sacrifice His life for His loved ones when He said: *«"Greater love has no one than this, than to lay down one's life for his friends."» John 15:13* However, he openly declared that he would die, rise again and will come shortly afterwards, when He said: *«"A little while, and you will not see Me;* (speaking here of his death) *and again a little while, and you will see Me"»* (And here He speaks of His resurrection and the beginning of His appearances as a sign of His resurrection from then forward and until His final coming) *John 16:16*

Even the angels testified about what Jesus said of His death and resurrection, when they asked:

«".. «Why do you seek the living among the dead? He is not here, but is risen! Remember how He spoke to you when He was still in Galilee, saying, 'The Son of Man must be delivered into the hands of sinful men, and be crucified, and the third day rise again.'»" Luke 24: 5-7

The Bible also testifies of the crucifixion of Jesus and His death:

«"Then he delivered Him to them to be crucified. So they took Jesus and led Him away. And He, bearing His cross, went out to a place called the Place of a Skull, which is called in Hebrew, Golgotha, where they crucified Him, and two others with Him, one on either side, and Jesus in the center."» John 19: 16-18

I wonder why Jesus endured all these pains and why He experienced death?

«"For God so loved the world that He gave His only begotten Son, that whoever believes in Him should not perish but have everlasting life. For God did not send His Son into the world to condemn the world, but that the world, through Him, might be saved. He who believes in Him is not condemned; but he who does not believe is condemned already, because he has not believed in the name of the only begotten Son of God."» John 3: 16-18

Jesus Christ still proves that He is alive today through miracles He carries out by the hands of His true disciples and messengers supporting His message through them *«"And they went out and preached everywhere, the Lord working with them and confirming the word through the accompanying signs."» Mark 16:20 «".. and many wonders and signs were done through the apostles." Acts 2: 43 «"Now God worked unusual miracles by the hands of Paul, so that even handkerchiefs or aprons were brought from his body to the sick, and the diseases left them and the evil spirits went out of them."» Acts 19: 11-12 «".. grant to Your servants that with all boldness they may speak Your word, by stretching out Your hand to heal, and that signs and wonders may be done through the name of Your holy Servant Jesus."» Acts 4: 29-30 «"... And through the hands of the apostles many signs and wonders were done among the people."» Acts 5:12*

«"Therefore He who supplies the Spirit to you and works miracles among you, does He do it by the works of the law, or by the hearing of faith?"» Galatians 3: 5

So, dear reader, do you believe that Jesus Christ is alive and appears today as He did in the past?

Yes, He lives! He appears today as unchanging evidence of His resurrection from the dead as it is written *«"Jesus Christ is the same yesterday, today, and forever."» Hebrews 13: 8* Any doctrine that contradicts this teaching is strange and not of God, even if the teachers claim that they are Christians and leaders of Christian churches and denominations that are false for the Holy Spirit witnesses in the verse directly after, saying: *«"Do not be carried about with various and strange doctrines. ...,"» Hebrews 13: 9* declares them to be strange teachings about Jesus.

Experiencing the appearance of Jesus in the church before me.

One day, I was in my local church, around 2014, and I strongly felt the presence of the Lord during praise and worship that was held on Sunday morning. My eyes were closed and I was completely focused on the Lord, when I suddenly saw Lord Jesus walking a few steps to the pulpit and opening His arms. I opened my eyes, bewildered at that the scene, wondering how it could be that I had seen the Lord in all His glory, white as snow and bright as a ray of sun walking on the platform of the church among those who stood there, perhaps not seen by anyone who stood beside Him, but certainly they felt His presence strongly among them. At the time, I talked to my wife and told her that I had seen Lord Jesus in a miraculous vision walking on the platform of the church, with His arms wide open. Two years later, near the end of July 2016, with that scene still in my mind, I felt an immense need for something greater than just occasionally reading the Bible, going to church and volunteering for some services for the Lord, the church and other Christian activities. I prayed a lot and I told the Lord how much I needed to see Him and meet Him personally here on Earth before I die. I wasn't fully aware of what I was asking, because all I felt was that the Christian life that I was leading was far less than what it was supposed to be. I felt that Jesus died for much more than just attending weekly church meetings and a few traditional Christian practices we were used to. I said, very hungrily, to the Lord, "Lord, is this all Jesus dies for on the cross? Isn't there something greater than this, rather even more than just leading a traditional, boring, and ordinary Christian life?" I said these words knowing that Jesus' blood that was shed on the cross deserves far greater than just to live a normal dull Christian life, limited by the walls of the church. While I was meditating on these thoughts, I received a phone call from someone I hadn't previously met asking me to translate a Christian book from English to Arabic. As we talked, I asked him, "Where did you get my number from?" He answered, "From your website on the Internet". I had indeed created a web page with my contact info as an interpreter of Christian books from English to Arabic. I had not updated that page for more than two years. No one had contacted me before about translating through that site at all except this person, and it is my nature to be a little cautious when dealing with Christian teachers who compose and write Christian books. The first thing I do, is check and test the teaching of the book which I would translate to make sure that it does not contradict the word of God - the Bible. If it is contrary in teaching to the word of God, I would immediately refuse to translate it because I do not want to be a partner of false teachers and counterfeiters lurking within the churches today, since I already have a bad experience in regards to this field, and which I will write about in another book, after this one, to discuss the true church and the false church as well as teachers and messengers who are sent by Jesus Christ and those who creep in like the devil to destroy and distort its image as well as how to distinguish between the two. Also, I will speak of how that had a negative influence on my life and my journey with the Lord until He redeemed me as it is written, *«"then the Lord knows how to deliver the godly out of temptations and to reserve the unjust under punishment for the day of judgment,"»* **2 Peter 2: 9** I encourage you, dear reader, to obtain that book as well later. After I talked to that person, I asked him for a copy of the book to go over well enough and make sure that this minister is sent of Lord Jesus as it is written: *« "Beloved, do not believe every spirit, but test the spirits, whether they are of God. Because many false prophets have gone out into the world."»* **1 John 4: 1** and so I learned to examine and check everything to take hold of only what comes from the Lord *«"... Test all things; hold fast what is good."»* **1 Thessalonians 5:21** I know for a fact that the Lord has given me the gift of discerning spirits as well as distinguishing people, as I received from the Lord the ability to discern what is of Him and what is not after many years, even when things seem to be from the Lord at first, because I believe in words the Spirit spoke through the Apostle Paul, «*"And this I pray, that your love may abound still more and more in knowledge and all discernment, that you may approve the things that are excellent, that you may be sincere and without offense"* *Philippians 1: 9-10*» And so, that person sent me a copy of a book called "Face To Face Appearances From Jesus" By the Author and Apostle David E. Taylor. After studying the book and making sure what was written as well as the examination of the author and the source of the teachings, the Lord declared to me that I had met His most cherished friend on Earth in modern times, i.e. the Apostle David J. Taylor. He has already proven that he left everything to follow the Lord and devoted his entire life to Jesus Christ and the message of the kingdom of God on Earth in our generation. The Lord has selected him to be, as Moses was in the Old Testament, a prophet of face-to-face experiences with the Lord, as Jesus appeared to him personally in His glorified body which He gained after His resurrection from the dead more than 1000 times over 20 years. He has been captured to heaven many times, and Jesus has shown him God the Father seated on His throne in heaven among several other things just as He did with the great Apostle

Paul when he wrote *in 2 Corinthians 12: 1-4 «"I will come to visions and revelations of the Lord: I know a man in Christ who fourteen years ago —whether in the body I do not know, or whether out of the body I do not know, God knows. such a one was caught up to the third heaven. And I know such a man—whether in the body or out of the body I do not know, God knows —. how he was caught up into Paradise... "»* The Lord then reminded me of what happened to me in prison about 13 years ago when he appeared to my Muslim cell mate and spoke to me of this man's release and the Lord said to me, emphasizing once again that He is still alive, and He constantly appears face-to-face. My connection to the ministry of Apostle David Taylor, called "Joshua Media Ministries International" - www.joshuamediaministries.org, has given me hope again that Jesus is still working in the midst of the church in His full glory with the same force he worked through in the past. I had began to lose hope in the church as a result of what I experienced in various Christian communities, most of which had squandered God's true power and took hold of guise only as religious Christian doctrine free from the presence of the living Christ and His face-to-face interaction with human beings in our present day. I personally, strongly experienced the presence of God in the Apostle David J. Taylor services and witnessed the signs and miracles as well as the power of God and His real presence in the meetings held in Michigan and across different countries of the world.

I thank the Lord because He arose a person like David in our day and age, and I encourage you, dear reader, to contact his service, whether online - and / or to go and attend the services and meetings that favor the appearance of Jesus in His glorified presence in front of the audience. Many are those who have experienced and still do this face to face meeting with Jesus because of this ministry as evidence for this generation that Jesus Christ is alive today and that He has risen from the dead. Praise the Lord.

I felt the strong presence of the Lord a second time in my local church during praise and worship for it is written: «*"But You are holy, Enthroned in the praises of Israel."*» *Psalm 22: 3* However, I did not see Him but I felt Him moving passionately on the platform of the church heading towards the left of the pulpit. So, I opened my eyes to see what will happen as He walked in that direction, and one of the musicians fell to the ground, kneeling, and crying from the intensity of the presence of the Lord, who walked toward him and touched him. He could not catch his breath, so he bowed kneeling with his head toward the ground in the presence of the living Lord in the midst of His living church.

One other day, I spoke with the pastor about my vision of Jesus in His glorified body and he replied emphasizing that he had seen His face on the pulpit one day so clearly that he took a picture of the visible face of Jesus in one corner of the pulpit just as the pastor was giving his message that day. Jesus told him that He was with him, and so, encouraged him to continue his service. I believe that Jesus is alive in the midst of true and lively churches that He has selected for Himself to be glorified through on Earth. He proves this sometimes through the clearly angelic appearance in the church before everyone to glorify Jesus Christ, the son of God in the midst of the living church. Praise God.

«"when the trumpeters and singers were as one, to make one sound to be heard in praising and thanking the Lord, and when they lifted up their voice with the trumpets and cymbals and instruments of music, and praised the Lord, saying: "For He is good, For His mercy endures forever," that the house, the house of the Lord, was filled with a cloud, so that the priests could not continue ministering because of the cloud; for the glory of the Lord filled the house of God.""» 2 Chronicles 5: 13-14

Finally, I say to you, dear reader, just as the apostle Paul said to his disciple Timothy: *«"Consider what I say, and may the Lord give you understanding in all things. Remember that Jesus Christ, of the seed of David, was raised from the dead according to my gospel,"»* **2 Timothy 2: 7-8**

May the Lord bless you and keep you from all evil for the glory of His eternal name.

"Now if Christ is preached that He has been raised from the dead, how do some among you say that there is no resurrection of the dead? But if there is no resurrection of the dead, then Christ is not risen. And if Christ is not risen, then our preaching is empty and your faith is also empty. Yes, and we are found false witnesses of God, because we have testified of God that He raised up Christ, whom He did not raise up—if in fact the dead do not rise. For if the dead do not rise, then Christ is not risen. And if Christ is not risen, your faith is futile; you are still in your sins! Then also those who have fallen asleep in Christ have perished. If in this life only we have hope in Christ, we are of all men the most pitiable. But now Christ is risen from the dead, and has become the first fruits of those who have fallen asleep. For since by man came death, by Man also came the resurrection of the dead. For as in Adam all die, even so in Christ all shall be made alive. But each one in his own order: Christ the first fruits, afterward those who are Christ's at His coming. Then comes the end, when He delivers the kingdom to God the Father, when He puts an end to all rule and all authority and power" 1st Corinthians 15: 12-24

The word of God is alive, effective and real in the lives of every believer - The first time I effectively used the word of God as a weapon in my life ... When I was about 20 years old, I remember being a shallow Christian despite serving as a deacon in the Catholic Church while living in sin at the same time. I had not experienced salvation or forgiveness of sins by the blood of Jesus Christ yet. I hung out with a group of friends that went to different places to have fun; spent our time in sins and bad relationships; and lived without a goal to look forward to. One day, we decided to go to one of the churches that we had not gone to before. Shortly after we entered the church, one of our friends came to me and told me that a brawl was about to occur outside the church gate with people who were not Christians because they had entered the church and harassed one of the girls praying inside. So I immediately went to see what will happen and found my friends gathered together confronting these intruders. I quickly went up to the one who seemed to be the leader and asked: "What exactly did you do to her?" He replied: "One of our comrades entered the church to pray, as well," I asked him: "What is his relationship with this girl and why did he harass her during prayer? Would you accept it if someone did that to one of your sisters?" He replied: "If anyone dares to touch my sister in such a way, I will do such and such to him," I felt great zeal what he had done in the house of the Lord (the church) as it is written: «*"... Zeal for Your house has eaten Me up."*» *John 2:17* And we engaged them in a violent fight that ended with an ugly and shameful defeat for them as they fled away although they outnumbered us and we would be considered foreign within their territory. I don't recall ever fighting with such jealousy, violence and force, not even remotely, except in this case because of the zeal I felt over what happened in the house of the Lord (the church). When we went to church, we received news that they are mobilizing a large group of young men carrying offensive hand-guns while we had nothing in our hands to confront them with. We were inside the church as they stood outside the church gate, waiting for us to come out and start the fight with whoever came with them. At the time, I was about 20 years old, and I had not experienced salvation through the blood of Christ yet, but I was jealous for the house of the Lord. The funny thing is, that before I went to church that day, I stopped by my buddy's house so we would go together to church, and I read a verse from the word of God on the wall in his house: «*"Call upon Me in the day of trouble; I will deliver you, and you shall glorify Me."*» *Psalm 50: 15* I remember thinking about that verse very well before we went to church that day. I don't know why it stuck to my mind that day or why I pondered about it. I never cared about it in the past when I had seen it on the wall in my friend's house. I did not take much attention to it, as all I knew at the time was that it was a verse from the Bible and that the Bible is the word of God. I believed that anything the Bible said had to be true even if I didn't understand it. I wouldn't doubt it at all because it was God who spoke and God never ever lied as it is written *«" let God be true but every man a liar ... "»* **Romans 3: 4** That verse remained in my mind even as we were going to church unknowing what we were going to face there that day.

When we entered the church after the violent fight was over, I stood and prayed to the God of the Bible and said to Him: *"Lord, you know I did not quarrel with these people but for one reason, a zeal for what they've done in your home. Now, you said call me in the day of trouble and I will deliver you and you will glorify me. So, here I am in a tight spot already, as all my enemies stand out there and are ready to harm me and my friends. You intervene and save me as You spoke."*

Back then, I believed every verse I read in the Bible without arguing because I knew that as long as God had spoken it then He would surely follow it through. I know that inside me very well.

After I prayed, the meeting ended and I received news that our enemies were raged with anger and ready to confront us as soon as we exited the church. I learned that there was around 30 people and we were less than 7, without any weapons. They carried knives and sharp tools with them, but they did not enter the church yard because of the large number of people there after the general meeting. So I had an idea and I told my friends: "Hey guys, we got into that fight for a good reason and they are the wrong ones entering the church, doing unworthy acts inside. So, let's go out together as one group, and if we glimpse anyone approaching us then we attack first and shred them to pieces. It won't matter what happens to us after that." So we all agreed on that as we had no other choice and they were like rabid dogs waiting for their prey, waiting for us to come out to them sooner or later as it is written « *"For dogs have surrounded Me; The congregation of the wicked has enclosed Me...."*» *Psalm 22:16* And so, we went outside as one group, and the moment we went out, we saw them flee over the side walls and fences of nearby houses, hiding without knowing what happened to them. We were amazed at what was happening. That minute, a taxi driver stopped directly in front of us and said: "Do you want a ride home?" I answered, "Of course we do", we got into the taxi and said to the driver, "Drive off as fast as you can, and if anyone stops you, don't!" He said, "Very well." As he was driving away, we looked back to see why they had escaped like mice, and we saw two police cars had entered the area heading towards the church. They heard that a bloody fight with sharp weapons was about to take place. It turned out that the pastor had called the police and we didn't know. So, we only knew that they had fled in fear, when they had in fact seen the police coming toward the church. We really did escape this bad situation and the Lord saved us from the hands of evil men that day, just as He declared to me earlier. It really was a miracle that we survived these evil men. Praise the Lord.

«"Let Israel now say— "If it had not been the Lord who was on our side, When men rose up against us, Then they would have swallowed us alive, When their wrath was kindled against us; Then the waters would have overwhelmed us, The stream would have gone over our soul;. Then the swollen waters would have gone over our soul". Blessed be the Lord, Who has not given us as prey to their teeth. Our soul has escaped as a bird from the snare of the fowlers. The snare is broken, and we have escaped. Our help is in the name of the Lord, Who made heaven and earth."» Psalm 124

That stayed with me to this day, because I learned that what God says in His word, the Bible, is real. He is faithful and honest in His words. When I believed the verse I read in my friend's house before we left to church, I activated the power of that word and brought it to life to deliver me from a day of trouble, which I wasn't aware of. If it hadn't been for the living word of God and my faith in it, that would have been the end of my life and the lives of those with me. It is said that the word of God is living and active. Glory be to God for His word remains true forever.

In this story, I do not encourage quarrels for any reason whatsoever as that was before faith in Christ as my personal Savior. Although, even after I received salvation, I still suffered a lot from anger bursts, but the Lord still works at my character to make me become more like Him. If it wasn't for the salvation of the Lord, I would be one of the most prominent leaders of terrorism in the world. But Jesus saved me, and changed my future as well as my eternal destiny. Today, He opens His arms to accept anyone who comes to Him in repentance and asks for forgiveness, to be changed from a destructive human being to mankind into a new human being in the same manner He changed Saul of Tarsus. Saul persecuted Jesus Christ and His followers wherever they were, but he was transformed into the apostle Paul. He did the same with me and He will do it with you as well, glory to His name.

A variety of practical tests accompanied by biblical verses from the word of the Lord.
«".. "I have put my trust in the Lord GOD, that I may declare all Your works."» Psalm 73: 28

I'll tell you, dear reader, to the best of my ability, of a few practical and diverse experiences, accompanied by the verses that speak of the validity and truth that the word of God is effective and alive in my personal life and all our lives as believers of the Bible, the word of God, here on earth...

A testimony to the literary living experience of *«"He guards all his bones; Not one of them is broken."» Psalm 34: 20*

While I was reading the word of God, after I received salvation during the beginning of 2000, and literately keeping the word of God in my heart, as Scripture says « *"Your word I have hidden in my heart,..."*» *Psalm 119: 11* I was meditating on the prophecy spoken about how God would preserve all the bones of Jesus « *"He guards all his bones; Not one of them is broken."*» *Psalm 34: 20* And since we are in Christ Jesus, all the promises given to Him are also given to us who are in Him. One day, while I was working in a factory that produces mechanical parts and machines that form metal, I was arranging the various metal pieces in their designated places, when suddenly one of the heavy metal pieces fell from a height of two meters on my left hand and specifically on three of my fingers. I felt like I an electric shock went through my hand and all over my body, and I experienced part of the pain that Jesus endured during the crucifixion all the while the verse « *"He guards all his bones; Not one of them is broken."*» *Psalm 34: 20* strongly echoed in my mind. I quickly withdrew my hand and held it tightly to my chest as the pain surged through my entire being. But the Lord gave me strength to endure the pain. The manager, a friend of mine, hurried towards me asking, "Are you okay?" I answered him, "Yes, I'm okay," feeling enormous pain. He rushed me to the emergency room because he saw with his own eyes what fell on my hand and the damage that took place. One emergency room refused to assist me in any way when they saw my hand. They said it looked like it had multiple fractures and they didn't want to take responsibility for anything until the X-ray showed how many fractures there were. So my friend quickly took me to a specialist but it took us two hours to find his clinic while I was in that condition. When he took a look at my hand he confirmed that there were multiple fractures and had an X-ray done. When the results came back, he asked in amazement, "May I conduct the examination of your hand again, because it seems that there is something wrong with the result of the X-ray?" I replied, "Of course," So the specialist performed a second X-ray on my hand and came back with the same result saying to my friend, "Are you sure that the metal piece which fell on his hand was of this size, this weight and from that height?" We said, "Yes" and the specialist replied, "Such a case usually only ends in cutting off at least two fingers, but according to the x-ray, your injured hand looks much better than the unharmed one", the specialist was shocked and couldn't believe what he saw to the extent that he said it was a miracle ... Praise the Lord.

Dear reader, I have in fact experienced the Lord literally preserving my bones because of His word. Not only did I witness it myself, but others saw that Jesus did and still does work in my life.

The Word of God truly is living and active in the life of whoever believes ... Praise the Lord.

A testimony to the verse, « *"He shall cover you with His feathers, And under His wings you shall take refuge. His truth shall be your shield and buckler! You shall not be afraid of the terror by night, Nor of the arrow that flies by day!"* » *Psalm 91: 4-5* And « *"For in the time of trouble He shall hide me in His pavilion; In the secret place of His tabernacle He shall hide me;..."* » *Psalm 27: 5*, And *"... I am your shield ..."* *Genesis 15: 1*, And *"Adonai is my strength and my shield. My heart trusts in Him, and I was helped"*, *Psalms 28: 7.*

One day, during the war in 2003 in Iraq, the fighting was severe, intense and fierce between Iraqi forces and allied Arabs against the United States. One of the more violent ground clashes which included the use of heavy artillery between the two forces was near where I lived at the time in the center of the capital, Baghdad. When the fighting stopped, I went along with a group of neighbors and friends to see what happened near the clash site. Suddenly, both sides began to open fire on us with machine guns. As we were running to flee the location, one of them threw a shell or bomb towards us. I ran away as fast as I could, but the sound of the bomb was deafening and it felt like it was getting closer to me. Instantly, I saw a bright white fireball almost as big as a football before my eyes. It came from the back and fell right in front of me as I was running with all my speed. It exploded in a spot, where if I had taken one step further, it would have landed on my head. When it exploded, I stopped in my tracks as if paralyzed and quickly started to check my chest to see if I was hit by anything. I continued to run quickly to hide with the rest of my friends and neighbors at a neighbor's house as they continued shooting at us. There were many neighbors who hated me for my faith in Jesus, and they saw a stream of blood from the direction which I ran from and said, "That is Fadi's blood right there. The bomb went off right in front of him." «*"All who hate me whisper together against me; against me they devise my hurt. "An evil disease," they say, "clings to him. And now that he lies down, he will rise up no more."»* **Psalm 41: 7-8** when we entered the house, the owner's wife, a specialized nurse in medicine said, "The shell landed right in front of you. The blood must be streaming from you." As she examined me, she asked, "Do you feel pain in any of your body parts?" I said, "No," as she continued, "It may be that the wound has not cooled yet, and you don't feel it because the shrapnel are still too warm in your body," Suddenly her husband shrieked in pain holding his leg. We looked, and the blood was pouring out of him not me, although he was the closest person to me but about 40 feet away from the explosion. One of the shrapnel had penetrated his leg and torn it apart. The bomb exploded in front of me but nothing harmed me. The question here is, why not?

Here, dear reader, are the details of what happened then...

The moment that the shell exploded, in a split second, I saw two huge wings that looked like hands quickly shield me, covering me from the fragments of the explosion. I saw them very clearly but they were transparent like glass. I would see the fragments of the shell fly around me in every direction, violently slamming and piercing into the walls of the houses on my right and left. I will never forget the sound of the blast and the sounds of the fragments pounding into everything around me, but it was as if they were running into an invisible barrier in front of me and bouncing off to a different direction without touching me.

Yes, dear reader, it was truly the hand of God which protected me that moment. I was supposed to be torn into pieces because of that explosion and those fragments. And everyone who hated me because of my faith in Jesus said, "There really is someone out there who protects you." This was shortly after I was released from prison for my participation in sharing my faith in Jesus with others. When my enemies saw that, their perception about me and my faith in Jesus completely changed. « *"Let them be ashamed and brought to mutual confusion who seek to destroy my life; Let them be driven backward and brought to dishonor Who wish me evil."*» *Psalm 40: 14*

A literal testimony of the verse *«"You have hedged me behind and before, And laid Your hand upon me."»* **Psalm 139: 5**

One day, while I was in church, I decided to sit somewhere I don't usually sit. In the center front row. No one was there yet. While I was praying, face down, I strongly felt the presence of the Lord to the sense that felt Him stand behind me. I felt, a hand gently laid on my right shoulder from the back, and I knew and realized that it was the Lord. I did not lift up my face to see who it was, because I knew that it was Lord Jesus, praise His name. The hand was raised quietly from my shoulder as I felt that He was with me and I was encouraged. I lifted my eyes and I looked back but I didn't find anyone standing behind because no one would put his hand on me in the church where I was sitting then. It really was Jesus encouraging me by His presence, the living God forever and ever. As the Psalm says *«"You have hedged me behind and before, <u>And laid Your hand upon me</u>"»* Praise the Lord, Alleluia.

A literal and living testimony of the verse *«"Who redeems your life from destruction,..."»* **Psalm 103: 4**

A testimony of how I literally was saved from the pit...

One day, back when I was in school, it was continuously raining heavily for three days in a row in Baghdad, to the extent that all the streets were flooded with water knee high, making it difficult even for car traffic in most streets. I decided to go to school even though the school bus did not come that day because of the rain. My school was about three and a half miles away from home, which is about an hour and a quarter walk, but it took me more than three hours to reach the school that day. A few minutes before I got to school, I entered a street submerged with water up to knee height. A car was parked deep in that yellow muddy water, so I decided to continue along the same path when a strong wave of muddy water hit me but with an electric stun. I jumped out of the water, bouncing back like a bird in the air several meters high and fell covered to my head with water. When I raised my head from the water, another wave came towards me and electrocuted me again. Again, I was thrown in the air and fell back into the water. I quickly got up and ran back in the muddy water and chose another route to get to school. When I got there, I didn't find anyone at school except two or three people at the time. No one had come that day because of the rain. So I left the school to go back home, a trip that would take a few hours more in that rainy weather. I decided to take a different route than the one I came through. While I was walking in that muddy water, I can't say why, but I suddenly stopped and started off another road that I had never taken home before. I knew that it was a much longer route and opposite to the way my house was, but I continued down that flooded street and got home in a desperate state a few hours later.

The testimony is this; two or three days after the rain stopped, the level of water in the streets was low and life returned to normal. I went to school as usual taking the street which I was electrically shocked twice. I found a thick set of electrical wires that were cut with large metal heads emerging from them where I was electrified before. They had thousands of volts written on them as they were the area's supply network of electrical power. The wires had been cut and neglected. When it rained and the water covered them, they easily became a conductor which made me fly into the air twice when I was stunned. I shouldn't have just died, but become a piece of coal being electrified with thousands of volts. Glory be to God who saved me from such a lethal strike that day.

Then, dear reader, I came back down the same street and saw the spot where I suddenly stopped, without knowing why, and changed my path as I told you before. To my surprise, I saw what had happened and I was shocked by the scene. A deep hole was left by reconstruction workers, filled with electrical wires that were cut and which had metal emerging from them. When it rained, it completely covered that hole that day. So when I suddenly stopped one step away from that pit and changed the path I was taking, I wasn't aware that I would have fallen into a fatal hole. I stopped and took a longer route that was opposite to my house's direction without knowing why.

The Lord caused that change of mind and I didn't realize the reason for it at the time, but I learned it later.

Glory to the Lord Jesus who literally redeemed my life that truly would have ended in a deep pit filled with cut electric cables ... Glory to the Lord. I am thankful for His love and compassion towards me.

A testimony to a nearly sunken ship...

I have also experienced, like the Apostle Paul, a nearly sunken ship, *Acts 27*.

One day, while I was traveling on board an enormous vessel through the Red Sea on my way to Egypt where I resided for almost 5 years, a malfunction occurred and it took from morning to evening to fix it. We should have set for the Egyptian ports in the morning but it took us until the evening to head out because of this sudden disruption. As the ship was sailing and approached the port which it should have stopped at, the transmitter in the Egyptian port warned the ship from approaching the port because of gusts of dangerous storms which horrifically moved the ship with violence in the middle of that dark sea that we couldn't see anything through. I stepped up on the deck of the ship and the strength of the storm almost pushed me to the sea. I held as hard as I could to the realms and prayed, "Lord, I pray that nothing should happen to this ship or anyone on it just as the Apostle Paul was on a ship that nearly drowned but didn't because he was on it and You were with him."

Dear reader, I prayed that prayer for one reason and that is because I had read the word of God, the Bible. Had it not been for the word of God which I kept in my heart, I wouldn't have known what to pray at the time. I would have been as frightened and terrified as the others on board that ship. Everyone was terrified in the night as we all looked at the deadly red fish with sharp teeth around the ship waiting for it to sink and have their feast of drowned human meat. We could see them with ship lights reflecting the panorama on each side.

After I prayed this prayer trusting that the Lord will deliver that ship, I remembered that Jesus Himself ordered the storm to calm down when He and His disciples were on board a boat. So I rebuked the wind to subside as Jesus, our teacher and greatest role model, did. *«"Then He arose and rebuked the wind, and said to the sea, "Peace, be still!" And the wind ceased and there was a great calm."» Mark 4:39* Glory to the word of God as it has been revealed again and activated to bring the results it usually does. The wind gradually died down until it was completely calm. The administrator on the Egyptian port transmitted a message which all the passengers heard, declaring that the sea had calmed down and the storm was over. Our ship could now safely enter the harbor with a group of small boats that were sent to help us at the time.

Dear reader, read the Bible and trust everything in it, because you never know when you'll need the word of God to deliver you in distress. When you remember the word of God, you activate it by speaking it in faith. It is living and active and able to deliver you and those around you. Praise the Lord and His Word, the Bible.

If you are not a believer in Jesus Christ as your personal Savior, I advise you to read the four Gospels; Matthew, Mark, Luke and John, and then faith will be generated in your heart as it is written: *«"... but these are written that you may believe that Jesus is the Christ, the Son of God, and that believing you may have life in His name."» John 20:31*

However, if you are a follower of Jesus and you were born of God through faith in what Jesus has done for you on the cross, I advise you to read the Bible, starting from the book of Acts to the Book of Revelation because it is your new identity in Jesus Christ. Persevere in doing this for many years until you are fully knowledgeable of Jesus and the Holy Spirit, and until you are filled with the grace of salvation given to you in the New Testament, which is yours by the blood of Jesus. When you are filled with the knowledge of God's grace, then, you can read the Bible from the beginning to the end without stumbling in comprehension. It is very important that you know your identity in Christ as you read what was before Christ. May the Lord grant you understanding in everything you read.

In the field of family life and marriage...

A testimony to the healing of my marital problems...

To be honest and frank with you, dear reader, I must admit that I have been through a lot of difficulties and hardships in my life at all levels, including my marriage. A huge part of which, was due to the lack of knowledge about what the Scriptures say about marriage; Another reason would be my personality, which I have personally suffered from as it is still in the process of change; And finally because of the war that Satan aroused to destroy marriages in general and mine in particular. Not to mention many other factors as well...

My marriage, especially in its early years, was very difficult as I have previously said. Marriage in general is continuously under satanic attack, as the devil's goal is to destroy marriage, the value of marriage, and the purpose of marriage; making it completely distorted through circumstances, people around us, ungodly opinions, the media and other weapons used by him and his associates on Earth. Thus, achieving his objective and destroying the entire family as well as the children and generations to come. This is exactly what the devil tried to do with me as he took advantage of my ignorance of the word of God about marriage and family. I am still learning to this day and I am continuously in the process of growth in this area.

One day, during that dark period of my marriage, I read in the Word of God verses related to everyday marital and family life such as:

«"For if a man does not know how to rule his own house, how will he take care of the church of God?"» Timothy 3: 5

«".. But if anyone does not provide for his own, and especially for those of his household, he has denied the faith and is worse than an unbeliever."» 1 Timothy 5: 8

«"Husbands, love your wives, just as Christ also loved the church and gave Himself for her,"» Ephesians 5:25

Those verses were from the word of God among others that had great effect over me, penetrating deeper and deeper into my soul. They showed me what I was like: the contrary of what the Word of God wanted me to be. Those words had such an influence on my way of thinking at the time, to the point that it changed my mind on many things that I was wrongfully doing against my household. I began to say to myself that I shouldn't treat my wife and my family in such an ungodly manner. Hence, the change began and my relationship with my wife began to take a different path. My way of thinking changed and with that my marriage and family changed as well, transformed from moving from bad to worse into becoming better and better. Glory to the Lord and His Word, the Bible, which was and still is transforming what we cannot change ourselves.

On employment ...A testimony of therapy for the issue of my work and my disability... When I was young, I used to lift weights and practice martial arts for a number of years. I was unbearably fierce and violent because of what I would see and hear in the community that I lived in - not to mention what I watched in the mainstream media, in addition to the electronic games I engaged in, without knowing it will all gradually shape my character into the person I was. This was before I became a child of God through faith in Jesus Christ our Lord. I was probably practicing weight lifting the wrong way as I relied on my personal unqualified knowledge, which ultimately affected my back when my spine and neck were injured as a result. I suffered pain in my back and neck for nearly 18 years, and when I immigrated to the United States, the first jobs I got required standing for long hours and lifting heavy objects. My back and neck pain kept increasing to the point where I could not continue to work. Finally, as a result to this disability, I stopped working for almost two years and nine months. I wasn't able to accept many jobs because of my disability and I depended on a few simple gigs here and there. My financial status was very bad and I was forced to stop working when a doctor informed me that my disability wasn't guaranteed to be reversible even through spine surgery, rather it would be a risk.

I was extremely frustrated back then, being a family man with the need to work and support my family while suffering at the same time from a disability which prevented me from doing that. In the meantime, as usual, I was seeking the word of God, the Bible. Some verses would come to my mind every now and then, such as:

«"But we command you, brethren, in the name of our Lord Jesus Christ that you withdraw from every brother who walks disorderly and not according to the tradition which he received from us. For you yourselves know how you ought to follow us, for we were not disorderly among you; nor did we eat anyone's bread free of charge, but worked with labor and toil night and day, that we might not be a burden to any of you, not because we do not have authority, but to make ourselves an example of how you should follow us. For even when we were with you, we commanded you this: If anyone will not work, neither shall he eat. For we hear that there are some who walk among you in a disorderly manner, not working at all, but are busybodies. Now those who are such we command and exhort through our Lord Jesus Christ that they work in quietness and eat their own bread."» 2 Thessalonians 3: 6-12

«"I have coveted no one's silver or gold or apparel. Yes, you yourselves know <u>that these hands have provided for my necessities, and for those who were with me</u>. I have shown you in every way, by laboring like this, that you must support the weak. And remember the words of the Lord Jesus, that He said, 'It is more blessed to give than to receive.'"» Acts 20: 33-35

«"For you remember, brethren, <u>our labor and toil; for laboring night and day, that we might not be a burden to any of you,</u> we preached to you the gospel of God."» 1 Thessalonians 2: 9

«"<u>Six days you shall work,</u> but on the seventh day you shall rest; in plowing time and in harvest you shall rest."» Exodus 34: 21

«"... <u>Man goes out to his work and to his labor until the evening.</u>"» Psalm 104: 23

And many other verses that encourage work. So I asked the Lord with all my heart, talking to Him about these verses, and about my disability that prevented me from doing what I should do. I prayed, and I also asked some brothers and sisters who attend a wonderful ministry to pray with me to get a suitable job for my health condition. I would like to mention the name of this ministry and thank them, Andrew Wommack Ministry – Website: www.awmi.net. In less than two weeks, as I recall, I got a job that I didn't know much about its details at the beginning. I was only told that it was in the field of transportation. I didn't know all the details, but the official told me it requires approximately 10 working hours a day driving a bus to transport passengers. I became depressed because I knew very well that I couldn't continuously sit for 20-30 minutes at all because of my injury, not to mention a difficulty breathing caused by the pain when I sometimes decide to sit for long stretches without a break. My mind was preoccupied with the idea that I was unable to sit too long in my condition, while at the same time thinking I couldn't stay out of work any longer. So I decided to take that job without thinking much about what would happen next. I decided to let the word of God work in my life in the area of work from then on *"...at Your word I will let down the net", Luke 5: 5*. I took the job and began training, daily working 16 hour stretches. As

I worked day in- day out, 6 days a week, morning to evening, as the Bible says, and not according to the world. The world always goes against the word of God; some work five days a week and others 7 days a week to make a living (It is the way we humans are, the majority rebel against God and His word, the Bible, and all you have to do is observe the miserable results. *«"Fools, because of their transgression, And because of their iniquities, were afflicted."» Psalm 107: 17* I decided back then to follow the Bible's teaching because I believe I am not more intelligent or wiser than He is or His word for that matter. Praise the Lord. Day after day, as I was busy, I suddenly remembered that I suffered from back pain and neck pain that would prevent me from sitting for long hours, and I realized that I had been healed of the pains I had suffered for so many years without even focusing on them. The Lord, *«"He sent His word and healed them, And delivered them from their destructions."» Psalm 107: 20* After a while, I came to realize the full details of this job and it was a transport service for the ill and disabled. The Lord transformed the evil that had happened to me into good, and the curse that was afflicted on me into a blessing. I was transformed from a semi-disabled man to a person who can help transport disabled people. One day, as I was conveying one disabled person who later became a friend of mine, we had a discussion. He was sitting in the back seat of the bus and I said, "I should have been sitting there in that back seat with someone else drives this bus. The Lord healed me and gave me strength to recover and has employed me, someone who should have been disabled, to transport the disabled. Glory to His name." Thanks to the Lord and His word, the Bible, for the wonders it does in our lives and in the lives of all who read and believe what it says. Nothing is too difficult for the Lord as it is written, «*"But He said, "The things which are impossible with men are possible with God."»* Luke 18:27

More testimonies will come in a later published book because the word of God is forever living and active.

Thank God for His word, the Bible, for everything it constantly does in our lives. Hallelujah.